Psychology of Addictive Behaviour

AIM HIGHER WITH *PALGRAVE INSIGHTS IN PSYCHOLOGY*

Psychology of the Media

978-0-230-24986-8

Psychology of Addictive Behaviour

Antony C. Moss and Kyle R. Dyer

978-0-230-27222-4

Anomalistic Psychology

Nicola J. Holt, Christine Simmonds-Moore, David Luke and Christopher Franch

978-0-230-30150-4

Research Methods and Statistics

Ian Walker

978-0-230-24988-2

The Psychology of Relationships

Julia Willerton

978-0-230-24941-7

Biological Rhythms, Sleep and Hypnosis

Simon Green

978-0-230-25265-3

Issues, Debates and Approaches in Psychology

Ian Fairholm

978-0-230-29537-7

Intelligence and Learning

Nick Lund

978-0-230-24944-8

Sport Psychology

David Tod, Joanne Thatcher and Rachel Rahman

978-0-230-24987-5

Forensic Psychology

Adrian J. Scott

978-0-230-24942-4

Adolescence and Adulthood

Leo Hendry and Marion Kloep

978-0-230-29640-4

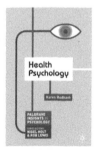

Health Psychology

Karen Rodham

978-0-230-24945-5

Phobias

Heather Buchanan and Neil Coulson

978-0-230-29536-0

Gender

Leonne Franklin

978-0-230-30273-0

To find out more visit **www.palgrave.com/insights**

Psychology of Addictive Behaviour

Antony C. Moss
and Kyle R. Dyer

PALGRAVE
INSIGHTS IN
PSYCHOLOGY

SERIES EDITORS:
NIGEL HOLT
& ROB LEWIS

palgrave
macmillan

First published 2010 by
PALGRAVE MACMILLAN

Palgrave Macmillan in the UK is an imprint of Macmillan Publishers Limited,
registered in England, company number 785998, of Houndmills, Basingstoke,
Hampshire RG21 6XS.

Palgrave Macmillan in the US is a division of St Martin's Press LLC,
175 Fifth Avenue, New York, NY 10010.

Palgrave Macmillan is the global academic imprint of the above companies
and has companies and representatives throughout the world.

Palgrave® and Macmillan® are registered trademarks in the United States,
the United Kingdom, Europe and other countries.

ISBN: 978–0–230–27222–4

This book is printed on paper suitable for recycling and made from fully
managed and sustained forest sources. Logging, pulping and manufacturing
processes are expected to conform to the environmental regulations of the
country of origin.

A catalogue record for this book is available from the British Library.

A catalog record for this book is available from the Library of Congress.

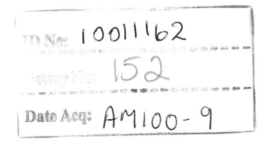

For Cheryl,
My best friend.
Also for Mum, Nick and Adam, Nan and Grad.
And Tange, for letting me go first.
TM

For Monika, Mahli and Mr B.
KD

Contents

List of figures

List of tables

Preface

Understanding addictive behaviours is a task that requires a willingness to expose oneself to an extremely broad range of theories and ideas from multiple disciplines, including psychology, pharmacology, medicine and allied health. Addictive behaviours touch every aspect of an individual's life: physical health, emotional wellbeing, relationships, and jobs. As such, theories that attempt to explain and understand the phenomenon must also reflect an appreciation of the diverse causes and serious consequences of addictive behaviour. Such diversity not only reflects the complexity of addictive behaviour, it also makes this an interesting and important health-related behaviour for us to study.

In this text we have tried to present a coherent picture of addictive behaviour by considering the key biological, psychological and social theories. There are, as you will find, a wide range of different perspectives on addictive behaviour, both in terms of understanding its development, and also in specifying its treatment and methods of prevention. The theories we present in this book are those we consider to have had the most impact on understanding and responding to addictive behaviours. However, the majority of the models and theories we present have not always been able to explain all the different biological, psychological and social domains of addictive behaviour; much remains to be understood before we can truly believe that we have a unified theory in this field.

A key goal of this book, therefore, is to present a new model which we have developed to provide a unifying framework for understanding addictive behaviours, both in acute situations (such as during a single drug-taking session) and during the experience of psychological and physical dependence. Our model conceptualizes addictive behaviours as having biological, psychological and social determinants and effects that can be moderated by cognitive processing, but incorporates key elements of many of the previous theories and models. We have built this model upon the twin pillars of pharmacology and cognitive psychology. By so doing, we feel that our model provides a map for those new to the area of addictive behaviours to help understand the key factors leading to its development and those that make it so difficult to treat, and to identify new avenues of research and policy development.

We would like to thank Nick Moss for his invaluable help in preparing the images presented throughout this book. We would also like to thank Professor Ian P. Albery for his input in developing the book's content and structure, for proofreading earlier drafts, and for his input in the development of the new model presented in the final chapter.

Antony C. Moss and Kyle R. Dyer

Note from series editors

When we make our own decisions about what we consume and in what quantities, we may feel that we are in control. Research suggests that a number of things influence whether or not we become addicted to gambling, alcohol or drugs, and the psychology surrounding this important area is discussed eloquently by Moss and Dyer in this book.

Antony C. Moss is a Senior Lecturer at London South Bank University. Kyle R. Dyer has twenty years' experience teaching and conducting research on illicit drug dependence and is a Visiting Fellow at South Bank University. Their research covers many aspects of the effects of drugs, drug dependence, testing and addiction including neurocognitive impairment, management of withdrawal and dependence. Together they make a formidable and extremely accomplished writing team.

- *If reading this book in preparation for your university study*, you will be looking for a good introduction to your chosen degree. This may be in any number of health-related or social fields, or it may be in psychology. The material here is relevant in all these areas and can help you extend significantly the material covered in your introductory texts.
- *If reading this book while at university*, you will no doubt be doing so as part of your recommended or wider reading, either for your course or in preparation for coursework. The book provides a well-thought-out navigation through this often poorly organized, and therefore difficult to understand topic. It is designed either as a replacement for your core texts or as support for them. The writing and editing team are keenly aware of the books available in this area

and have been careful to write a book that complements or replaces what is currently available. As such, it will form a useful addition to your bookshelf.

- *If reading this book as you study for pre-university courses such as A-level*, you will be only too aware of the quantity of work mounting up around you. Both teachers and students will find this book written with their requirements in mind. It provides the material you need while maintaining that important extension that helps you keep one step ahead of the rest. The Reading Guide at the end of the book tells you where different A-level specifications appear.

Whether studying medicine or sociology, psychology or social care, you will find the material herein relevant and, more importantly perhaps, interesting and even useful. In an age of excess where additive behaviours are only too easy to engage in, Moss and Dyer demystify many of the relevant theories and provide a learned, but fascinating read.

Nigel Holt and Rob Lewis
Series Editors

Chapter 1

What is addictive behaviour?

👁 Introduction

Addictive behaviours are challenging – they can affect anyone, they develop slowly, often without our awareness, they touch all aspects of our lives, and they can be very difficult to treat and prevent. Throughout this book we will present the theories, evidence and ideas, drawn from the fields of psychology, pharmacology, medicine and allied health, that are most useful for understanding addictive behaviours. The purpose of the present chapter is to introduce some of these key ideas, issues and arguments, and provide a foundation for understanding the rest of the book. We use the term *addictive behaviours* to capture not only **drug** and alcohol dependence (both physical and psychological), but also to include other behaviours, such as gambling, internet and sex, that people can become dependent upon. While at times there may be a focus on drug dependency in this text, it is important to remember that some key concepts apply to all addictive behaviours, and not just those that involve the administration of a drug.

In this chapter we will examine:
- Issues in defining addictive behaviour
- The clinical criteria used for diagnosing dependence disorders
- The distinction between physical and psychological dependence
- The role and implications of the disease concept in addictive behaviour
- Pathways out of addictive behaviour

◉ What is addictive behaviour?

It's as good a way as any to begin a book with a question. However, the question we have chosen to open with – What is addictive behaviour? – does not have a straightforward answer. The problem with defining addictive behaviour is that, while it is a term that most people understand in a broad sense, it covers so many diverse behaviours: alcohol dependence, drug dependence, smoking, and gambling, to name but a few.

At first, trying to pick a definition that is specific enough to be useful, but broad enough to incorporate this diverse range of behaviours that we think of as examples of 'addictive behaviour' would seem like a tall challenge. The fourth edition of the Diagnostic and Statistical Manual of Mental Disorders (DSM-IV-TR) (American Psychiatric Association, 2000), which is used by clinicians to identify and diagnose 297 recognized mental health disorders, does not in fact mention 'addiction' at all. This is because the term addiction implies a medical illness and does not adequately incorporate the biological, psychological and social components of this disorder. Instead, the DSM-IV-TR uses the term Substance Dependence (see Box 1.1). The key symptoms identified are tolerance; withdrawal; increased use over time; inability to cut down use despite a desire to; preoccupation with obtaining and using, or recovering from the effects of a drug, and giving up of other interests and activities in favour of use; and continued use despite obvious harms. These criteria are a good starting point for understanding addictive behaviour, so let's think about each in turn.

Box 1.1: DSM-IV-TR Criteria for diagnosis of Substance Dependence (American Psychiatric Association, 2000)

A maladaptive pattern of substance use, leading to clinically significant impairment or distress, as manifested by three (or more) of the following, occurring at any time in the same 12-month period:

(1) Tolerance, as defined by either of the following:
  (a) a need for markedly increased amounts of the substance to achieve intoxication or desired effect
  (b) markedly diminished effect with continued use of the same amount of the substance
(2) Withdrawal, as manifested by either of the following:
  (a) the characteristic withdrawal syndrome for the substance (refer to Criteria A and B of the criteria sets for Withdrawal from the specific substances)

(b) the same (or a closely related) substance is taken to relieve or avoid withdrawal symptoms

(3) the substance is often taken in larger amounts or over a longer period than was intended

(4) there is a persistent desire or unsuccessful efforts to cut down or control substance use

(5) a great deal of time is spent in activities necessary to obtain the substance (for example, visiting multiple doctors or driving long distances), use the substance (for example, chain-smoking), or recover from its effects

(6) important social, occupational, or recreational activities are given up or reduced because of substance use

(7) the substance use is continued despite knowledge of having a persistent or recurrent physical or psychological problem that is likely to have been caused or exacerbated by the substance (for example, current cocaine use despite recognition of cocaine-induced depression, or continued drinking despite recognition that an ulcer was made worse by alcohol consumption)

Specify if:

With Physiological Dependence: evidence of tolerance or withdrawal (that is, either Item 1 or 2 is present)

Without Physiological Dependence: no evidence of tolerance or withdrawal (that is, neither Item 1 nor 2 is present)

Reprinted with permission from the *Diagnostic and Statistical Manual of Mental Disorders*, TextRevision, Fourth Edition (Copyright 2000). American Psychiatric Association.

Tolerance

Have you ever noticed how coffee seems to affect you less if you have been drinking a lot of it lately? Perhaps you have heard someone being referred to as a 'hardened drinker'? Or perhaps you know of someone who has been taking pain medication for a chronic condition and has remarked, on a particularly bad day, that 'the tablets just don't touch the pain *any more*'?

Each of these examples is an instance of **tolerance**. Simply put, tolerance to a drug means that, over time and with repeated use, larger doses are required to achieve the initial experience. So you need to drink more coffee to feel as you did when you first started drinking it; you find you can drink more alcohol without becoming as disoriented; or you may need stronger doses of painkillers to relieve your discomfort. So, tolerance is the first key characteristic of drug dependence. The biological basis of tolerance will be explained further in Chapter 2.

Withdrawal

People like sugary foods, some more than others. Those of us who do like sweet treats will know what is meant by the phrase 'sugar rush'; that heady feeling of overindulgence that accompanies eating an ice cream dessert-for-two by yourself, or downing a packet of sherbet in one. And those of us who have ever had a sugar rush will also know what it is like a short while after the 'buzz' has worn off – we feel groggy, lethargic and even a little depressed. Quite the opposite of the effect the sugar had on us in the first instance. This is withdrawal: a negative state that occurs when we cease using a substance. Importantly in the context of addictive behaviour or substance dependence, taking the substance will immediately lead to a reduction in withdrawal symptoms, and this can motivate continued use. Tolerance and withdrawal together represent **physical dependence**, and the **neuroadaptation** that occurs in response to a drug (see Chapter 2).

Addictive behaviours develop slowly

Few, if any, problem drinkers ever began their drinking career with two bottles of vodka a day. Instead, alcohol dependence is marked by a progressive increase in consumption over time – until consumption has reached levels that most social drinkers would find quite astonishing. This increase in consumption over time is linked to the two phenomena mentioned above: tolerance and withdrawal. As an individual uses alcohol more and more, they become more tolerant to its effects, and will experience increasing negative effects of withdrawal whenever they are not using.

These two factors of tolerance and withdrawal are important in understanding why drug use can increase to such dramatic levels – with problem drinkers consuming three or four times a social drinker's weekly average consumption every day, and heroin users administering doses that would have caused an overdose early in their drug use career. Interestingly, the same pattern of recreational use developing into problem use as a function of time can be seen in other addictive behaviours (for example gambling).

Preoccupation with obtaining and using, and giving up other interests

Many people can relate to the feeling of becoming a little obsessive about certain activities; be it the keen amateur footballer who attends Sunday League matches and training come rain or shine (or hail, or snow, or thunderstorms), or the *Big Brother* obsessive who cannot stand to miss a night's viewing. When we develop particular interests in life, we often find ourselves restructuring our other daily activities to accommodate our passions, and this is quite normal. In the case of dependence, however, the tendency to value the 'passion' over other things may often end up well out of any reasonable proportion, such that personal relationships, employment, and even family commitments may be neglected in favour of obtaining and using a drug, or recovering from its effects.

Neglect of important areas of one's life to focus upon the addictive behaviour will inevitably lead to problems – our relationships may break down, we may lose our jobs and our health will suffer. These problems are often the most debilitating aspects of an addictive behaviour, and ironically the stress that they cause can actually lead people to turn to further engagement in the behaviour. The problems caused by addictive behaviours in turn become motivators, strengthening the addictive behaviour. Moreover, these problems can be the most difficult to deal with, and have significant effects not just on the individual, but on those close to them and the wider community: addictive behaviours impact upon us all.

Continued use despite obvious harms

So some people love football, others enjoy *Big Brother*. But surely, if a visit to your GP led to the startling revelation that continued engagement in playing/watching would lead to your untimely death, you would think that you would give up either activity in a heartbeat. You may be remorseful at the loss of a favourite pastime, but then life is more precious to us than any one hobby. However, among users of certain substances, including alcohol, such information – for example that continued drinking will lead to cirrhosis of the liver and premature death – often fails to halt use. Breakdown of marriages, loss of jobs, imprisonment and serious health problems are among the many other negative consequences often associated with substance dependence which seem ineffective in stopping use.

The picture of addictive behaviour that we have painted here looks something like this: a person might be said to be dependent if they demonstrate signs of increased tolerance to a substance, of withdrawal when they are not using, and whose life has become focused on obtaining and using their substance of abuse, despite the obvious fact (to themselves and those around them) that it is causing significant harm to their health and general wellbeing. However, we have been talking mainly about substance dependence disorders so far, and clearly we need a way of understanding non-substance-related dependence disorders, which can be as problematic for the individuals concerned as substance dependence disorders. Instances of dependence that do not involve substances differ from the examples discussed so far in that they do not necessitate tolerance or withdrawal. This brings us on to the final set of terms contained within the DSM-IV-TR diagnostic criteria.

Physical vs. psychological dependence

Under the DSM-IV-TR (APA, 2000) criteria for diagnosing substance dependence, it is possible for an individual to have an addictive behaviour without either tolerance or withdrawal, but to still be diagnosed as dependent. This is an important point, as it then becomes possible to diagnose other dependence disorders (such as problem gambling or eating disorders) using these criteria.

The symptoms of problem gambling, which would include a preoccupation with the act of gambling and a tendency to continue gambling despite extremely heavy and unmanageable financial losses, certainly seem to fit the general model of addictive behaviour as we have been talking about it. The key distinction that has to be raised between dependence on behaviours such as problem gambling, internet or sex, and substances, such as heroin, alcohol or cocaine, is the absence of withdrawal and tolerance.

Thinking about the distinction between physiological and **psychological dependence** also raises an important question about how we should think about addictive behaviour. Take, for example, the clinical observation that a patient in a coma can develop both tolerance to medication, and experience a withdrawal syndrome when the medication is stopped (that is, physical dependence). But this does not necessarily mean that they will want to continue use beyond the illness – that is, they have not developed psychological dependence.

The implication here is that addictive behaviour comprises psychological dependence, which can be long lasting and difficult to treat, and physical dependence, which represents physical neuroadaptation, is often short term, and is somewhat easier to treat. This has important implications for how we think about addictive behaviour itself, which guide not just how we treat it, but also how society deals with it. To illuminate this point, we shall now ask three questions which will set the scene for the rest of this book.

👁 Is addictive behaviour a disease?

This may sound like a fairly simple question, with a fairly obvious answer. It would be tempting to just say, 'Of course it is! What else could it be?', and leave it at that. However, life and addictive behaviours are not that simple, and whether we consider addictive behaviour as a disease or not will have important consequences upon how we judge the person, and what treatments or sanctions society might utilize in response to it. At its simplest, a disease can be considered an abnormal condition that impairs bodily function and has specific signs and symptoms – that is, it implies an illness or a sickness.

Think about it like this: if addictive behaviour is a disease, what does that say about the role of the individual who has the disease? If you happen to catch influenza, to what extent are you responsible for getting better? Of course, you are responsible for making sure you heed the advice of your GP – taking your medication, resting properly, eating plenty of healthy foods and maintaining hydration. But our question about responsibility cuts deeper than the extent to which you are responsible merely for trying to get better. What we really mean here is, to what extent could you simply make the choice to not have flu any more? This now sounds like a slightly inane question – the answer is of course that we have no choice! If we could simply choose ourselves out of experiencing the symptoms of the influenza virus, we doubt there would be any more cases of flu from here onwards. So a disease state, in ordinary usage, seems to imply that the individual *has an illness* that they cannot simply decide not to have any more.

Let's apply this idea of a disease to alcohol dependence, as an example. Does it make sense to talk about someone having the 'disease of alcoholism' which causes them to drink excessively, beyond the point of enjoyment? If, like Jellinek in his seminal 1960 book *The Disease Concept of Alcoholism*, we decide that alcohol dependence is a disease, what precisely is it that we are saying the person 'has'? Jellinek's view was that the disease of alcoholism was essentially a loss of control over drinking behaviour – he also argued that not all 'alcoholics' are in fact diseased alcoholics, because many people who drink problematically are able to exercise control over their actions (so-called functioning alcoholics). Critics of the disease model, ourselves included, argue that the evidence basis that any addictive behaviour ever involves a total loss of control is very weak, but more importantly has dramatic ramifications both for the individual and for those whose role it is to provide treatment and support. Furthermore, it is extremely important that we remember that the individual will always have a role in the development of their addictive behaviour, and also their treatment and recovery from it. The stigma of labelling addictive behaviours as a disease, it has been argued, can lead to individuals feeling like unwilling victims of their condition, for which they rely on others to overcome.

An important issue, therefore, when deciding whether we believe that addiction is a disease or not, is what role the individual and the environment play in the development and maintenance of addictive behaviours. We all agree that the flu victim cannot just stop themselves having the flu, any more than a cancer patient can decide that they will now go into remission and begin recovering from their unfortunate condition. But something nagging remains about addictive behaviour: the alcohol dependent patient who has been attending a local treatment group, having remained 'dry' for the last six months, finds themself at a crossroads when offered a drink by a new acquaintance. They can both accept it, and possibly risk a relapse, or refuse, and continue on the path of abstinence that they have been on for the last six months. There is something about this situation that doesn't seem apparent in the case of flu, cancer or migraines: *choice*. If the problem with the flu is the influenza virus that has entered your body, then the problem with alcoholism is *the act of picking up a drink, and then another*. So what we need to decide, then, is to what extent a person is or is not in control.

Our discussion so far has helped to bring into sharp relief the issues surrounding the idea of 'addictive behaviour as a disease'. These issues are all important, and should not be ignored. However, one must also keep in mind that we should not reject the 'disease concept' simply because it is unpalatable. If evidence were presented to show that addictive behaviours are the result of an identifiable disease state, we would have to treat this seriously. Leshner (1997) wrote an article entitled 'Addiction is a brain disease, and it matters'. In this paper, Leshner put forward the argument that addictive behaviours are a form of brain disease because all forms of drug dependence involve structural and functional changes in a common region, the 'reward pathways' (which we will discuss in more length in Chapter 2). According to Leshner, it is this common underlying problem that allows us to think about addictions as a disease. On the other hand, other influential perspectives in the field have been developed which argue that the disease approach is simply not helpful, and serves to shift focus away from what addictive behaviours actually are.

Orford (2001; 2002), for example, has argued that there are too many similarities between non-drug-related addictive behaviours, such as gambling, 'sex addiction' and 'internet addiction', for us to meaningfully conclude that there is a common underlying biological pathway which is central to understanding addictive behaviours. As MacLeod (2002), in a review of Orford's seminal book *Excessive Appetites*, put it:

> Sometimes, in relation to physical withdrawal syndromes for example, neurochemistry is relevant. However, in general, this thesis eschews the idea that [addictive] behaviour is best understood in terms of brain chemistry simply because everything human beings do, think or feel has a neuro-molecular correlate. (MacLeod, 2002, p. 118)

Whether you take the view that the root of addictive behaviour is fundamentally biological or not, the important thing to keep in mind is this: none of these views suggest that biology is totally unimportant, nor do they suggest that social or psychological factors should be sidelined. Indeed, the patterns of use and even some of the effects of taking certain drugs of dependence can be culturally dependent (see the Thinking scientifically box below). Rather, debates in this field focus on how broadly we can and should define addictive behaviour, and whether it is possible or even desirable to treat it as a disease.

Thinking scientifically →
The cultural dependence of dependence and use

It has long been understood that the effects of drugs such as alcohol on behaviour, and indeed the way in which they are used, are highly dependent upon social influence. For example, MacAndrew and Edgerton (1969) have described two societies, the Paraguayan Abipone

Indians and the Peruvian Vicosians. The former are depicted as a gentle people, lacking in aggression toward one another, until they become intoxicated. The result of alcohol consumption is said to be excessive violence, often resulting in fatalities. Conversely, the latter are described as being no more or less violent when inebriated, instead displaying greater sociability. The intention of this comparison is to cast doubt upon the idea that alcohol is in some sense able to alter behaviour in a direct way. Instead, alcohol-related behavioural change is more appropriately understood as being the result of locally defined customs, norms and expectations.

Other historical examples, which remain relevant today, provide insights into how drinking patterns, for instance, can be closely defined by the social group to which one belongs. In the time of Alexander the Great, who died in 349BC, patterns of binge drinking behaviour, governed by social norms and expectations, have been described as follows:

> One of the companions, elected by his fellows as leader of the symposium and called *symbiosarches*, arranged the rules of drinking (when and how much everyone should drink) which all the guests obeyed. Usually the companions elected the most hardened drinker, whose demands were considerable; thus, the consumption was excessive ... (Liappas, Lascaratos, Fafouti and Christodolou, 2003, p. 564)

This extract provides several important insights about the way in which alcohol was used during these ancient times, and is made more interesting given the amount of media coverage given to problems around binge drinking in recent years.

Is addictive behaviour a choice? Can you 'Just Say No'?

Trying to put ourselves in the shoes of our imagined individual in the example above, who is trying to decide whether to accept or refuse an offer of a drink after months of abstinence: does he or she have a choice in this situation? Let us assume that they decide to take one drink, but that they don't stop there, and find themselves experiencing a full-blown relapse. This is a common experience for many individuals with dependence. Our question here requires us to decide whether, in that instant, our imaginary friend could have 'just said no'; would it have been that easy? Common sense might tell us that the choice is obvious, and they did have one, but chose the wrong path. Of course, the alcohol did not get into their stomach without them picking up the drink – alcohol, or other drugs for that matter, cannot 'decide' to get into a person's bloodstream, any more than a roulette wheel can put a bet on for you, or a cigarette can buy itself from an off-licence, jump into your unsuspecting mouth, and light itself up. A choice is obviously being made by the person to pick up and drink that drink, or light up and smoke that cigarette.

So does any of this matter? As a matter of fact, it does. If we were to suppose that addictive behaviour is a disease in the traditional sense of the word, we would also have to argue that individuals do not play any part in their own addictive behaviour. The disease made them do it. If, on the other hand, we decide that there is always some element of choice involved in addictive behaviour, we start to view things a little differently. We begin to see that individuals can help themselves; that they can choose not to use. But in the same way that viewing dependence purely as a disease can lead us to underestimate the role of the person in their own recovery, viewing dependence as a matter of choice can take us in another problematic direction. If engagement in addictive behaviour is a choice, why don't dependent individuals just sort themselves out and stop using? After all, treating and dealing with the consequences of addictive behaviour costs societies huge sums of money each year. Should we have much sympathy, or money to fund treatment services, for people who are just being a bit irresponsible? Of course things are not that simple. When we suggest that there is some element of choice in addictive behaviour, we are not trying to suggest that it is *nothing more than a choice*: instead, try to think about addictive behaviour as being an instance of having a very difficult choice to make. In later chapters we will explore in some detail the various factors that can make this choice (to abstain from using or doing the addictive behaviour) more or less biased against the best interests of the individual.

Various models have been developed in the field of health psychology that are premised on the idea that a number of different factors can influence an individual's intentions to behave in a particular way. Two of these models, the theories of reasoned action and planned behaviour, are summarized in the Thinking scientifically box below. In the next chapter, we will be focusing on the physiological aspects of addictive behaviours which strongly influence an individual's choices. For instance, given that alcohol withdrawal syndrome is life-threatening, it is hard to argue that an alcohol-dependent individual has any choice to not drink, if no medical support were available to deal with their symptoms during a period of abstinence.

Thinking scientifically →
Social cognitive models applied to dependence

Ajzen's (1991) theory of planned behaviour (TPB) was derived from Fishbein and Ajzen's (1975) theory of reasoned action (TRA). The fundamental distinction between the TRA and TPB was that the latter was developed to account for behaviours that are not necessarily under an individual's conscious control. The TPB, illustrated in Figure 1.2, suggests that individuals hold beliefs about the expected outcomes of behaviours, as well as holding attitudes towards the perceived value of such outcomes (for example, what will happen if I stop smoking, and is this an outcome I desire?). These expectancies, and their importance for understanding addictive behaviours, are discussed in greater depth in Chapter 3. The TPB also suggests that behavioural intentions are affected by beliefs held by the individual about others' perceptions of certain behaviours (for example, if I were to stop smoking, what would others think, and am I motivated to comply with their views?). Perceived behavioural control in the TPB relates to how an individual feels about their ability to control a partic-ular behaviour (for example, do I think that I am able to maintain abstinence from smoking under, say, conditions of extreme stress?).

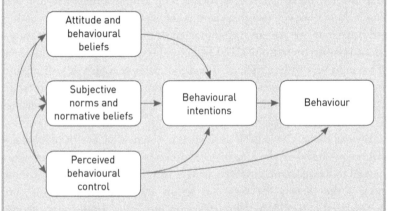

Figure 1.1 The theory of planned behaviour (based on Ajzen, 1991)

The TPB uses all of these constructs to make predictions about an individual's behavioural intentions, which are then used to predict actual behaviour, in areas such as drug use (McMillan and Conner, 2003) and risky sexual behaviour (Godin and Kok, 1996). However, a major caveat in this theoretical model of behaviour is that the link between intentions and behaviour is quite weak – in a recent analysis of over 47 experimental studies, Webb and Sheeran (2006) concluded that large changes in an individual's intentions would not produce correspondingly large changes in behaviour. Instead, the evidence suggests that changes in intentions are often met with changes in behaviour that are far weaker. One of the reasons for this, which we will explore in greater depth throughout Chapters 4 and 5, is that many of the processes that underlie our behaviour are not consciously motivated or available to individual self-report.

◉ What is the path away from addictive behaviour?

Theories of the development of addictive behaviour, which we will discuss throughout this book, are often very good at telling us how a person came to develop their pattern of addictive behaviour. Of equal, if not greater, importance is an understanding of how addictive behaviours can be prevented and overcome. In Chapter 6 we discuss the various interventions that are used to treat addictive behaviours. For now, it is helpful just to think about the various stages involved in changing behaviours like alcohol dependence or problem gambling. Here it would be useful to consider the stages through which a person might pass when trying to achieve abstinence from an addictive behaviour.

The transtheoretical model (TTM) (DiClemente and Prochaska, 1982) provides an intuitive description of the stages of change involved in addictive behaviours. The model describes five discrete stages through which an individual would pass when changing their behaviour, and in principle is supposed to be applicable to any form of behaviour change. Table 1.1 summarizes the five stages of change.

The TTM stages of change can be broadly divided in to pre-action (1–3) and post-action (4–5) stages. Progression through each stage is motivated by different factors, including things like social support, realizing that the current behaviour is harmful to oneself or others, or simply learning new information about the behaviour which was previously not known. It is also important to realize that an individual can potentially slide back to any of the previous stages during a process of change. For example, an ex-smoker in the maintenance stage who ends up relapsing may re-enter the stage of action (that is, they immediately stop smoking again), preparation (that is, they take proactive steps to rejoin a smoking support group but continue smoking until they get there), contemplation (that is, they decide that they will stop again within the next six months, but they do not take any steps to ensure this will happen), or even the precontemplation stage (that is, they simply continue smoking).

Stages of change	Explanation	Example
1 Precontemplation	The individual has no intention to attempt to change behaviour within the next six months	A *current smoker*
2 Contemplation	The individual has thought about changing their behaviour and intends to do so within six weeks	A *current smoker* who has decided that they will stop smoking later this year, but has taken no steps to begin the process of change
3 Preparation	The individual has thought about changing their behaviour and intends to do so within the next 30 days, and has begun taking steps to achieve this goal	A *current smoker* who has been to see their GP and has arranged to begin attending a smoking cessation support group
4 Action	The individual has changed their behaviour	An *ex-smoker* who has recently (within the last six months) quit smoking
5 Maintenance	The individual has changed their behaviour, and this change has been sustained for more than six months	An *ex-smoker*

Table 1.1 The stages of change (adapted from Prochaska, Redding and Evers, 2002)

One of the key criticisms of the TTM has been the lack of clarity about how individuals are supposed to move between stages – or more specifically, how therapists and clinicians can best support progression from one stage to the next (Sutton, 2001; West, 2005). The **protection adoption process model** (PAPM) (Weinstein and Sandman, 1992) is a very similar model to the TTM, but it divides the precontemplation and contemplation stages into four different steps. Figure 1.2 illustrates the differences between these two stage models.

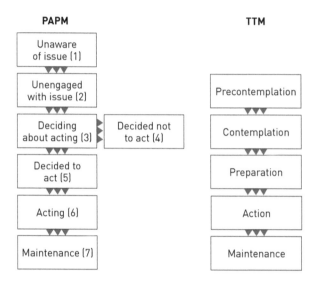

Figure 1.2 A comparison of the protection adoption process model (PAPM) and the transtheoretical model (TTM)

The PAPM is useful for two reasons: first it allows for the possibility that some individuals may be unaware of a need to change their behaviour (stage 1), or that they are aware of the need but simply are not motivated to consider changing (stage 2). This distinction is important, as, from a health promotion perspective, these two types of people would require different interventions (see Chapter 7). The TTM would consider both types of person as simply being in precontemplation about changing their addictive behaviour. Also, the model allows for the possibility that an individual may think about changing their behaviour, but decide not to act on the information. Again, this is important from a clinical perspective as it would be problematic to assume that every smoker who is not trying to quit is simply not fully aware of the dangers – often, people can be aware of a danger but simply decide to take the risk, perhaps because of a mistaken view that there is no personal risk of experiencing those harms.

Frankfurt (1971) proposed an interesting classification system for addiction, suggesting that an individual engaging in an addictive behaviour could be 'Wanton', 'Willing' or 'Unwilling'. *Wanton addicts*, to use

Frankfurt's terminology, are those who simply engage in their addictive behaviour without ever questioning whether it is right or wrong to do so. *Willing addicts* have thought about their behaviour, and decided that they will continue with it. *Unwilling addicts*, on the other hand, have thought about their behaviour, decided they would rather not engage in it, but find they cannot stop. This interesting trichotomy is relevant not just to the additional stages in the PAPM, it also highlights an important issue of the role of choice in addictive behaviour, which we will return to in Chapters 5 and 6.

The second benefit of the PAPM is that the authors of the model have made some explicit suggestions about how to help people transition from one stage to the next. These suggestions are summarized in Table 1.2.

Stage transition	Suggestion for promoting transition to the next stage
Stage 1 ↓ Stage 2	Education and tertiary prevention – make individuals aware that their behaviour may be damaging to themselves or those around them
Stage 2 ↓ Stage 3	Help people find reasons to care about changing their behaviour (that is, reduce ambivalence)
Stage 3 ↓ Stage 4 or 5	Understanding and challenging, where necessary, an individual's perceptions of their susceptibility to the health risks (for example lung cancer), the severity of the risk (for example death, chronic health problems), **self-efficacy** (for example whether they feel capable of changing), perceived barriers and social norms
Stage 5 ↓ Stage 6	Providing resources to help promote behaviour change, such as 'how-to' information, cues to action, assistance and support groups

Table 1.2 Suggestions for promoting stage transitions in the PAPM

There are many more models of health behaviour change, but the key message at this stage is to appreciate that changing an addictive behaviour, like any other behaviour, is a complex process that involves a lot of different factors. From simple things, like not being aware that smoking can cause lung cancer, to less obvious things, like challenging someone's belief that they are simply not 'strong willed' enough to overcome nicotine addiction, promoting behavioural change is a hard thing to do. It also requires an understanding of the particular behaviour that needs to be changed, as well as an understanding of the individual and their beliefs and motivations.

⊙ Summary of this book

We have started this book with a very general overview of addictive behaviours, discussing the diagnostic criteria used for identifying dependence (physiological and/or psychological), and have thought about what it means to change an addictive behaviour. In the following chapters, key issues in addiction will be discussed in greater detail, beginning with the biology of drug dependence in Chapter 2. Chapter 3 will then describe some of the oldest, and in many respects most influential, psychological theories of addictive behaviour, which developed in the **behaviourist** tradition of psychology. In the following two chapters we will focus on the importance of self-control (Chapter 4) and automatic or unconscious cognitive processes (Chapter 5) in understanding addictive behaviour. Chapters 6 and 7 will then present the ways in which addictive behaviours are treated and prevented, respectively. Finally, in Chapter 8 we will bring all this information together and present a new model of addictive behaviour. Our model conceptualizes addictive behaviours as having biological, psychological and social determinants and effects that can be moderated by cognitive processing. The model of addictive behaviour that we will present is our way of trying to show how one can think about the various aspects of addictive behaviour in a structured way, appreciating that the development, maintenance and treatment of addictive behaviour is influenced by a wide range of biological, psychological and sociocultural influences.

In reading this book you will no doubt discover that there is a lot to know about addictive behaviour, and that there is a lot we still need to know. At the end of each chapter you will find key readings that will be of interest to those wanting to know more about a particular area.

⊙ Further reading

Ajzen, I. (1991) The theory of planned behaviour. *Organizational Behavior and Human Decision Processes*, 50, 179–211.

Jellinek, E.M. (1960) *The Disease Concept of Alcoholism*. New Brunswick, NJ: Hillhouse Press.

Leshner, A.I. (1997) Addiction is a brain disease and it matters. *Science*, 278(5335): 45–8.

Orford, J. (2002) *Excessive Appetites: A Psychological View of Addictions* (2nd edn). London: John Wiley.

Prochaska, J.O., Redding, C.A. and Evers, K.E. (2002) The transtheoretical model and stages of change. In Glanz, K., Rimer, B.K. and Viswanath, K. (eds) *Health Behavior and Health Education* (4th edn). San Francisco: Jossey-Bass, pp. 99–120.

Chapter 2

The biology of addictive behaviour

👁 Introduction

Many addictive behaviours involve the administration of drugs such as alcohol, nicotine, heroin or cocaine. The effects of these so-called drugs of dependence have been studied extensively and we know much about the biological effects of these drugs on the body and brain. The brain is a complex organ that strives for balance, and whenever we introduce a drug to the brain we upset that balance. The brain will seek to adapt to redress this imbalance, by minimizing the effects of the drug. Furthermore, addictive behaviours that do not involve the administration of drugs still involve the release of endogenous chemicals (neurotransmitters) in the **reward pathway**. This in itself causes an imbalance which the brain will seek to counter. Understanding these processes is key to understanding addictive behaviour.

In this chapter, we will examine:
- The various ways in which drugs can enter the body
- The effects of a range of drugs of dependence on the brain
- The biological basis of drug tolerance and withdrawal
- The role of endogenous neurotransmitters in the development of dependence

History shows us that people have used and abused drugs since the earliest recorded times. Indeed, it would be hard to find any civilization throughout history that did not experiment with, use or abuse drugs which can cause dependence. The primary reason for this is that drugs have a number of sought after effects, which can enhance mood, alter consciousness, improve our performance on a task, remove feelings of discomfort, and make us want to take them again. It is only in recent times that science has begun to reveal how the brain operates, and how it adapts to the presence of a drug.

A drug can be defined as a chemical substance, with a known chemical structure that produces a biological and psychological effect when it is administered. Drugs can be obtained from plants or animals, they can be entirely synthetic or they may be the result of genetic engineering. The key factor is that to be a drug, it needs to be something that is administered to the body rather than a natural (endogenous) substance released by the body.

In order to understand how drugs affect us and why people continue to use them, we must first understand how they affect us biologically. The drugs of abuse and dependence with which we're interested all have their primary effects in the brain. They interact with cells within certain structures in the brain, and by so doing, they change our biological functions (like heart rate, blood pressure and sweating), how we feel and think (psychology) and how we act (behaviour). Most drugs will also have actions in other parts of the body, but for the drugs of dependence, the brain is the most important site of action.

Each of the drugs that we cover in this book has different effects upon us, different chemical structures and interacts with different parts of the brain. However, they do share some common characteristics, and it's these commonalities that can tell us so much about the harms that can arise from their use and indeed the nature of drug dependence itself.

A key point is that all the drugs of abuse produce a sought after or pleasurable effect; that is, they are rewarding to us in some way, either by providing a sought after positive effect or removing some form of discomfort. All the drugs of dependence will produce a positive emotional response by releasing a neurotransmitter called dopamine in the *reward pathway*, which is the part of our brain responsible for emotions. If those drugs can reach the brain quickly and effectively, because of either their chemical structure or how they are administered, then it is more likely that they will reinforce continued drug use and it is more likely that we may become dependent on that drug.

After repeated use of a particular drug, our brain will adapt to its presence in such a way that we may only feel 'normal' when the drug is present. We may find that we need to use more and more of the drug to achieve the sought after effect, and we may experience depression, anxiety and a range of unpleasant physical symptoms when we try to stop using the drug.

To understand the biological basis for these common effects of drugs of abuse, we must start by looking at what happens to the drug when it enters the body. We must consider how we take the drug – do we smoke it, inject it or drink it? These different **routes of administration** not only change how long it takes for us to feel the effect of the drug but also how intense those effects will be and how long they will last. Once administered, how does the drug reach the brain? These phases we call **absorption** and **distribution**. Finally, how does the amount of drug in our body change over time? The effects of the drug will eventually wane; the body will break down the drug molecules and remove it – these phases we call **metabolism** and **excretion**. All these stages of drug action affect patterns of drug use; how much we take, how often and how long is needed to recover from the effects.

It is also important for us to understand how the drug affects the function of the brain and changes our moods, thoughts and biological functions. The different effects produced by different drugs can be understood by examining which structures of the brain are affected by the drug and how the brain adapts to a drug's continued presence. Drugs that work on similar parts of the brain will also tend to have similar effects on biological functions, subjective experiences and behaviour.

Within the brain, drugs mostly work on proteins namely **receptors**, enzymes, neurotransmitter carriers and ion channels. Receptors are protein molecules that recognize and respond to endogenous chemical compounds called **neurotransmitters**, which send messages between the cells in the brain. Individual classes of drugs bind only to certain receptors, while receptors only recognize certain classes of drugs. Drugs may either increase or decrease the activity of structures and pathways within the brain.

Finally, if we take a drug on a continuing basis, the body will gradually adapt, leading to a reduction in the effect of the drug. This may possibly lead us to increase the amount and frequency with which we use the drug. Eventually we may find that we need to use the drug frequently just to feel 'normal'. These issues of **tolerance** and **physical dependence** on a drug are central to understanding the long-term abuse of drugs and addictive behaviour. Let us now begin by looking at how a drug enters the body, and how the body reacts to its presence.

◉ Routes of administration, absorption, distribution, metabolism and excretion

Routes of administration

In the context of the biology of drug abuse and dependence, drug effects can be understood by their action in the brain. It may be a long and complex process for a drug to reach the brain, or it can happen quite quickly. Obviously, the first step is for the drug to enter the body and depending on the chemical composition of the drug, there are a number of different possible methods which we call routes of administration. The following are common routes of administration for drugs of abuse:

- Oral – such as drinking a liquid or taking a pill
- Injection – injecting a drug into a vein (intravenous), into a muscle (intramuscular) or slightly under the skin (subcutaneous)
- Inhalation – inhaling the heated vapours of a drug or smoking it in the form of a cigarette
- Application to skin – such as applying an ointment, which is a method more common for some therapeutic medicines rather than drugs of abuse
- Through **mucous membranes** – that is, by sniffing a drug (intranasal) or holding a liquid in your mouth

The route of administration that is used will depend in part on the *chemical characteristics of the drug* and in part by *personal preferences*. Some drugs, such as those that come in plant form and are relatively unprocessed (for example tobacco, cannabis), can't be injected but can be smoked, snorted (for example snuff) or cooked and eaten. Other drugs are in the form of a gas or are highly volatile and so can be inhaled (for example volatile substances such as the vapours from glue or lighter fluid). Where drugs have more than one route of administration, the decision of which one to use is partly an issue of personal preference – for example, many people dislike the sensation of inhaling smoke, and so may opt to snort or inject a drug instead.

The chemical characteristics of some drugs limit the possible routes of administration. In some cases heat will destroy the drug and no effect will be felt (for example cocaine hydrochloride). However, if we can change the chemical structure of a drug (for example by removing the hydrochloride molecule to produce cocaine freebase, more commonly known as crack), it can then be heated and the vapours inhaled.

Many drugs come in the form of soluble powders. These drugs can be taken in just about any method we choose. An example here is heroin, which can be heated and the vapours inhaled (called 'chasing the dragon') or injected into the body. Injection is a very effective way of administering a drug and we will feel the effects very quickly. However, injecting a drug can be dangerous. Skin lesions and vein damage can occur if insoluble substances are mixed with the drug. These may be powders used to 'cut' the drug to be able to increase the amount that is sold. Similarly, tablets contain many substances beyond the drug and some of these are insoluble. If tablets are crushed and mixed with water to be injected, these insoluble substances can cause serious damage to the skin and blood vessels. Finally, if more than one person uses the same syringe, then various diseases such as hepatitis or HIV/AIDS can be spread.

The decision to use a particular route of administration can also be guided by the *speed with which the person wants the drug to act*. A drug will enter the blood stream, reach the brain and produce an effect most rapidly after the intravenous injection and inhalation routes of administration. Administering via mucous membranes (such as snorting a powder) is somewhat slower, while the oral route is the slowest of all, as the drug must first reach the gastrointestinal tract and then be absorbed into the bloodstream to reach the brain.

The difference in the time between these different routes of administration and producing an effect can vary from a few seconds to several minutes. Furthermore, the time that we can feel the drug effects will also vary according to which route of administration was used. In general, the slower the onset of drug action, the more gradual the build up of the effect and the longer it will seem to last. In Figure 2.1, we can see that after injecting a drug, the drug concentration rises rapidly and then falls away quite quickly. After swallowing a drug, the drug concentration rises more slowly and stays at a lower level for a substantially longer time. The importance of this relationship between routes of administration and peak drug effect is that the sooner an effect is experienced, the more reinforcing it is (see Chapter 3).

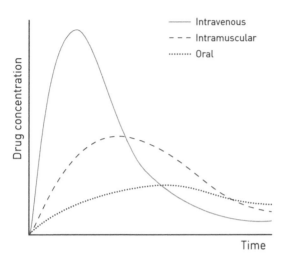

Figure 2.1 The time course of drug concentration and effect by different routes of administration (adapted from White, 1991)

Absorption

The drugs of abuse and dependence act in the brain. So to produce their effects they must journey from the site of administration to the brain by travelling through the circulatory system. The process by which a drug enters the blood stream after it has been administered is called absorption.

The differences in the time it takes for a drug to produce an effect can be explained in part by differences in the rates of absorption into the blood stream. Obviously the fastest way for a drug to enter the blood stream is to be injected directly into a vein or blood vessel (that is, intravenously). After intravenous injection, the drug travels immediately throughout the body via the heart and lungs (see *distribution*). For all other routes of administration, the drug needs to cross at least one barrier (cellular membrane, for example the walls of blood vessels) to reach the bloodstream.

The number and nature of the cellular membrane barriers the drug has to pass through depend on the route of administration, and obviously the more barriers that a drug has to pass, the longer it will take to reach the brain and the more likely that some drug will be lost along the way (see *metabolism*). We can think of these cellular membranes as hurdles over which the drug has to pass before it can reach its site of action within the brain. The drugs of abuse are quite good at passing these barriers, as they share some important characteristics. Let's look now at some of the factors that determine the speed and success with which a drug will cross these cellular barriers.

The first factor that impacts on the success with which a drug will pass through a cellular barrier is the degree to which it is *soluble in lipids* (fats). Each cell membrane consists mostly of lipids. So how easily a drug will move through a cellular membrane is determined by the degree to which the drug will be dissolved in the membrane lipids. Most gaseous drugs (for example solvents, anaesthetics) are highly lipid soluble, so the cellular membranes are easily passed (Rang, Dale, Ritter and Flower, 2007). Alcohol is another drug that is highly lipid soluble.

The second factor is the *degree of ionization* of the drug. An ionized molecule is one that has had either a positive or negative particle removed or added to it. In solution, a certain proportion of the drug molecules will ionize and become charged particles. The *ionized form of the drug is much* less *likely to cross the cellular membrane than the deionized form*. As such, the greater proportion of ionized molecules in the drug, the slower the rate of movement of the drug across the membrane.

The proportion of ionized molecules is itself affected by the relation-ship between the acidity or alkalinity of the fluids next to the membrane surface and the acidity or alkalinity of the drug itself (Rang et al., 2007). If there is a match there will be little ionization and so there will be rapid movement across the cellular membrane. However, if one is acidic and the other alkaline then there will be a high proportion of ionized mole-cules and so absorption will be slow. In general, alkaline drugs are most easily absorbed, and the drugs of abuse tend to be alkaline.

The *size of the drug molecule* will also affect the rate with which it is absorbed into the bloodstream. Drugs that consist of relatively small molecules will pass through the membrane faster than would be expected purely by their degree of lipid solubility. Similarly, the vehicle in which the drug is administered can also be important. For instance, some medi-cations can be administered in such a way as to release the active drug into the blood stream slowly over time. We see this most commonly with certain types of medicines: for example, antihistamines used to treat symptoms of hay fever can be obtained either in tablets that are taken 2–4 times a day, or as one-a-day preparations. These are the same drugs, but the one-a-day formulation is designed to release the active compound slowly over a 24-hour period.

The final factor that will affect the rate of movement of a drug across the membrane is *the difference in concentration of the drug on the two sides of the membrane*. The greater the difference in drug concentration on each side of a cellular membrane, the more rapid the movement – a process called *diffusion*, which is the same process that occurs when a sugar cube dissolves in a glass of water. While it might be tempting to think that the rate of absorption would start as very quick and then slow down as the concentration difference becomes equal, this is not the case. Once a drug has entered the blood stream, it is immediately carried away from the site of entry to other parts of the body (Rang et al., 2007; White, 1991). As a result, there is always a difference in the drug concentration either side of the membrane.

Box 2.1: Summary of factors affecting drug movement across cellular membranes

The factors of a drug which determine the speed and success that it will cross a cellular barrier include:

- Lipid solubility – more lipid soluble drugs *more easily* cross cellular barriers
- Degree of ionization – ionized drug molecules can *less easily* pass cellular barriers
- Drug molecule size – small molecules *more easily* pass cellular barriers than large molecules
- Concentration differences – the greater the difference in drug concentration either side of a cellular barrier, the *more easily* the drug will pass the barrier

---

With these factors in mind, let's look back at the different routes of administration and their impact on the rate of absorption. Obviously, a drug's entry into the blood stream is instantaneous after intravenous *injection* and so this route of administration has the fastest rate of absorption. After injecting a drug we may feel the effects quite quickly. The effects also may be more intense than if we had used a different route of administration.

Inhalation of vapours is the second quickest method for the drug to enter the blood stream. Inhaled drugs enter the lungs either as a gas or as tiny smoke particles. The lung is specialized for absorption; it has a very large surface area and blood passes through the lungs at a very rapid rate. At each point in the lung, only a single membrane separates the air space in the lung from the capillary (blood vessel). This feature of the lungs permits the rapid and easy entry of oxygen into the blood stream but it also works extremely well for drugs. The rate of absorption through the lung is also assisted by the rapid flow of blood around the lung. This means that the drug is quickly carried to other parts of the body and there is no build up of the drug near the lung. As such, the difference in drug concentration in the lung and in the blood stream remains very high.

Drugs that are in the form of gasses are also assisted in their absorption rate as they have high lipid solubility and a relatively small molecular size. For drugs that enter the lungs as smoke particles (for example nicotine from cigarettes), absorption is a little slower than drugs in a gaseous form, but still quite fast compared with some of the other routes of administration. Highly soluble drugs will quickly separate from the smoke particles, whereas less soluble ones will do so more slowly.

Drugs can enter the blood stream by *crossing mucous membranes such as those in the nose or mouth* (for example snuff or cocaine). The mucous membranes of the inside of the mouth and nose are composed of several layers of cells. Although these membranes are quite thin when compared with the skin, they will still create a much greater barrier than the single membrane barrier found in the lung. Blood supply to the nose and mouth is very rich and this will assist in absorption. To ensure the maximum possible drug effect, drugs taken by this route need to be kept in contact with the mucous membrane surface for enough time for all the drug to be absorbed. Experienced drug users who use this route of administration will learn to achieve this – for example, people who sniff snuff (a powdered form of tobacco) will learn to keep the snuff in their nose and delay sneezing (White, 1991).

Injecting a drug by the intramuscular or subcutaneous methods is rarely used outside medical contexts. However, people who have injected a drug intravenously for a number of years may find that their veins become damaged or collapse quickly when they try to inject a drug, and so they will have little choice but to change their route of administration to injecting into a muscle (intramuscular) or just beneath the skin (subcutaneous).

Absorption via these routes can be fairly rapid depending on the blood flow that is near the site of injection. If a drug is injected very close to a blood vessel, such as into a muscle, then only the wall of the blood vessel needs to be crossed for the drug to enter the blood stream. However, if the drug is injected into body fat, then it may take some time for the drug to move close to a blood vessel. Furthermore, the health of the individual is also important. For example, shock reduces blood flow, meaning that drug absorption via the intramuscular or subcutaneous routes can be quite slow in people who have been injured and are in shock.

The final and most common route of administration, but the route with the slowest rate of absorption, is the *oral* route. When we swallow a drug, it must first dissolve (if it is a tablet), and then travel through the stomach before it can be absorbed in the small intestine. While a small amount of the drug can be absorbed in the mouth and stomach, most of the drug will be absorbed in the small intestine – the time it takes for the drug to reach the small intestine will affect the rate of absorption and how long it takes for us to feel its effect.

The lining of the stomach consists of large folds that provide a large surface area for a drug to cross into the bloodstream. However, the contents of the stomach are highly acidic, and this leads to a high degree of ionization and the slow absorption of alkaline drugs, such as recreational drugs. As a result, the drugs that we are interested in are all primarily absorbed via the small intestine, so the time it takes to move through the stomach and into the small intestine dictates the rate of absorption. If a drug is taken on an empty stomach, it will pass through the stomach to the small intestine quite quickly. It's for this reason that people who drink alcohol will become drunk more quickly if they drink without having eaten than if they eat a meal before drinking – and also why people who are intending to drink heavily talk about 'lining their stomach' with a large meal before they drink.

The small intestine is specialized for the absorption of nutrients from food. It has a very large surface area and a high density of blood vessels. The environment outside the small intestine ranges from weakly acidic at one end of the intestine, to weakly alkaline at the other – so no matter what the acidity or alkalinity of a drug, there is always somewhere along the small intestine where a drug can be absorbed into the blood stream.

As we can see, there are a number of factors that can affect the rate of absorption of a drug into the blood stream, while, in turn, the rate of absorption can affect the time it takes for a drug to produce an effect and the size of the effect that is produced. The delay in feeling a drug's effect, and the intensity of the felt effects, can affect how rewarding (or reinforcing) the drug is and the likelihood that it will be taken again (we will discuss this more in Chapter 3). For now, we know that once a drug has entered the bloodstream, it must then move to the brain to produce its effect. So let's turn to this process of drug movement throughout the body.

Distribution

Once a drug has been absorbed into the blood stream, it then needs to travel throughout the body to reach the brain. During its journey, some of the drug may leave the blood stream and be stored in a body tissue, or it may be metabolized (see below), leaving less of the drug to reach the brain and have an effect. Eventually the remaining drug will reach the brain where it can finally leave the blood stream to connect with the brain and produce its effect. This process of drug movement is called *drug distribution.*

As a drug travels throughout the body it will come across a number of barriers, slowing its movement and gradually removing some of the drug from the blood stream. If no drug at all were to leave the bloodstream, the drug would eventually distribute evenly throughout the body and distribution would occur in just a few minutes. However, blood vessels are composed of cells (with the same properties described in Box 2.1) that form various roadblocks for the drug, slowing its entry into body tissues such as the brain.

The principles that we described affecting the rate of absorption, will also affect the degree and speed to which a drug is distributed. As such, the rate at which a drug will leave the blood stream and enter a body tissue depends on how lipid soluble it is, the size of its molecules, the proportion of ionized molecules and the existing concentrations of the drug in the plasma and the body tissue. A drug that can cross a membrane rapidly and easily will eventually be distributed throughout the entire body. Drugs that cross membranes less easily are less evenly and widely distributed. Furthermore, drugs will leave the bloodstream and enter various body tissues where they have little or no effect before reaching the brain. So, essentially, there is dilution, meaning that less of the drug reaches the brain than was originally administered.

When a drug does finally reach the brain, it faces a further roadblock called the **blood–brain barrier**. This consists of the cellular lining of capillaries in the brain. The blood-brain barrier makes it difficult for drugs to enter the brain, and is essentially a defence against chemicals and other foreign bodies. Drugs that contain large molecules, those that are ionized and those that are not lipid soluble, will all have difficulty crossing the blood–brain barrier (Rang et al., 2007; White, 1991).

A good example here is the differences in distribution and activity between heroin and morphine, two opiates with a long history of abuse in many societies. Heroin (diacetylmorphine) is a chemically manipulated derivative of morphine. In the body, it is rapidly metabolized to morphine, and the effects of heroin and morphine are virtually indistinguishable. However, heroin is more lipid soluble than morphine, and so it can cross the blood–brain barrier more rapidly and easily than morphine, producing a much greater effect. So, essentially, heroin is really just a way of packaging morphine, so that more morphine can cross the blood–brain barrier. In fact, heroin only lasts in the body for a minute or two, and the effects that people experience are actually the effects of morphine.

So to sum up, the rate of absorption of a drug into the blood stream is affected by the route of administration, the chemical properties of the drug, the conditions at the site of administration and individual health factors. Drugs are distributed through the body by the blood stream and diffuse across cell membranes. These membranes form roadblocks between different parts of the body, protecting it from what it may consider to be a foreign substance. In the case of drugs of abuse, the important barriers to cross include the lining of the gastrointestinal tract and the blood–brain barrier. To cross these barriers easily and quickly, drugs need to be lipid soluble, deionized, and relatively small in molecular size (see Box 2.1).

Before discussing the effects produced by the presence of a drug in the brain, let's first discuss how the body removes the drug, and terminates its effects, via processes called metabolism and excretion.

Drug elimination: metabolism and excretion

The processes of absorption and distribution take the drug from its site of administration to its site of effect, and in the case of the drugs of abuse that site of effect is the brain. Before we move to discussing how drugs produce their effects, we must first discuss the final processes involved in the body's reaction to a drug, namely removing the drug, processes which we call metabolism and excretion.

The body actively works to rid the body of the drug, if it didn't, then of course a drug effect would be indefinite. These two phases – metabolism and excretion – are how the body *eliminates* a drug and terminates its effect. Metabolism describes the way in which the body breaks down the drugs, making it easier to remove, and involves a chemical reaction within the body to form a product which is easily excreted. The metabolites formed (that is, the chemicals produced when the drug is metabolized) may themselves be active (that is, they can produce an effect in the brain similar to the original drug) or they can be inactive (that is, they do not produce a discernible effect). Excretion refers to the elimination from the body of the drug and its metabolites.

Drug excretion

There are a number of different routes by which the body will excrete drugs. These include via the lungs in expired air, or in bodily fluids such as sweat, saliva or urine.

For those drugs that are in the form of gases (for example nitrous oxide), the body excretes the drug by the lungs. To be excreted by the lungs, the same processes occur as for absorption, but in reverse. That is, the same membranes need to be crossed and the same factors as described above determine the rate at which this will occur.

Once in the lung, the drug is lost from the body each time we exhale. During the process of breathing, some of the drug is removed from the body using the process of diffusion across the mucous membrane of the lungs. The drug and its metabolites move back through the blood stream to the membrane of the lungs, and because the concentration of drug in the lung is zero, the drug moves across the membrane and is excreted as we breathe out. That is, the drug is lost through expiration: more of the drug will move from the blood stream into the lung until there is none left in the blood.

Interestingly, drugs such as solvents and alcohol are also partly excreted by the lungs. About 5–10 per cent of alcohol is excreted through the lungs in exhaled air, which forms the basis of breath alcohol tests. Breath alcohol tests use a chemical process to measure the concentration of alcohol in expired air. As we assume an equilibrium in alcohol concentration in the exhaled air and the blood, this measure can be used to estimate the concentration in the blood stream.

Drugs that are not gaseous at body temperature can't be eliminated through the lungs and so need to be excreted through a body fluid. There are a number of body fluids available including saliva, sweat, tears, mucous secreted from nose, urine, and in mothers, human breast milk (this is very important as it means an infant can receive the drugs taken by the mother through breastfeeding). The amount of drug that can be excreted by each of these fluids is directly proportional to the amount of that fluid that is produced and lost from the body each day. As the greatest volume of lost fluid is urine (we produce about a litre each day), most of the drug is excreted through urine.

Most drugs leave the body in urine, which is produced in the kidneys. One of the main jobs of the kidney is as a blood-filtering device. Blood constantly enters the kidney where molecules and chemicals of a certain size are filtered; the blood is then reabsorbed back into circulation with the products left behind forming urine. In very general terms, this filtration involves a cellular membrane (again with properties similar to those mentioned in Box 2.1). Deionized, lipid soluble drugs easily re-enter circulation, whereas those with molecules that are ionized or non-lipid soluble have some difficulty. As a result, drugs that have been *metabolized* to form ionized products will be most easily excreted from the body.

Drug metabolism

In many ways, the metabolism of a drug is no different to the process by which the body rids itself of foreign chemicals and toxins. If a drug is metabolized, it undergoes a number of possible chemical processes that transform the drug into a new compound. If that new compound is inactive then the action of the drug will be terminated. In some cases though, the product of metabolism is itself an active drug, which may have an effect very similar to that of the original drug. For instance, one of the products of heroin (diacetylmorphine) is morphine, and many long-acting benzodiazepines (for example diazepam) form a metabolite that is very similar in action to the original drug.

Metabolism can take place in a number of organs in the body but the most important is the liver. The liver has high concentrations of enzymes that produce a chemical reaction with drugs to form new products. One of the chemical reactions that can occur is that the enzyme will assist the drug to combine with another molecule (for example an amino acid) to produce an inactive drug that is highly ionized with low lipid solubility. In this form, the end product (or metabolite) can be easily excreted by the kidneys.

Together these processes of metabolism and excretion represent the body's attempt to rid itself of a drug, or what it considers to be a foreign object and waste product. The health and functioning of the liver and kidneys are therefore important for the effective clearance of a drug. One of the effects of long-term alcohol abuse is liver damage; as such, individuals who abuse alcohol may find that they take longer to eliminate alcohol from their body if their liver is not functioning properly. Similarly, elderly people cannot metabolize drugs as quickly as younger people, and this has to be taken into consideration when prescribing medications.

Drugs may also need to be transformed into products more easily excreted from the body. For instance, lipophilic (that is, soluble in fat) or deionized drugs need to be transformed into metabolites that are hydrophilic (that is, soluble in water) or ionized forms, to be more easily filtered by the kidneys. In total, metabolism and excretion will terminate the action of a drug and remove it from the body.

◉ Time-effect and dose-effect relationships

So far we have discussed how the amount of the drug at its site of action will change over time – increasing as the drug is absorbed and distributed and then falling as it is metabolized and excreted. The length of time it takes for a drug to stop producing an effect and leave the body is governed by many factors including characteristics of the drug and the form in which it is taken, the route of administration and the health and functioning of the body. While there are many factors affecting the length of time that a body will exert an effect, for this discussion we will limit ourselves to the key aspects of metabolism and individual variability.

The role of metabolism and excretion on drug concentrations over time

The rate at which a concentration of a drug will rise or fall will change over time. To begin with, absorption is quite rapid as there is a greater difference in drug concentration on either side of the membrane. The rate will then gradually slow as the concentration difference changes, and more of the drug is in the blood stream.

Similarly, metabolism and excretion also occur at a greater rate when the concentration of the drug in the body is higher and then gradually slow as the drug is eliminated. The rate of metabolism is initially faster simply because there are more drug molecules in the body; excretion will be faster for the same reason as for absorption, that is, there is a greater difference in drug concentration on either side of the membrane in the kidney.

There are exceptions to this and some drugs, such as alcohol, will be metabolized at a constant rate; these drugs require a particular enzyme to be metabolized and the availability of these enzymes is limited. As such, it takes a longer time to get rid of a larger dose as only a limited amount of the drug can be metabolized at any one time – alcohol is the best example here. Approximately 90 per cent of alcohol is metabolized by a chemical reaction in the liver. However, a particular enzyme called *alcohol dehydrogenase* is required for this process to occur. Humans can produce enough of this enzyme to metabolize approximately one unit of alcohol (approximately 8g of alcohol) each hour. As a result, blood concentrations of alcohol will fall linearly. This means that you can only get rid of approximately one unit of alcohol per hour, so when you drink at a rate that is higher than one unit of alcohol per hour, you will become increasingly intoxicated. It is nothing more than an urban myth that steps such as drinking coffee or eating after you have consumed alcohol will make you sober more quickly. The only thing that you can do to become sober is wait.

The processes of absorption, distribution and elimination do not occur independently. Once a drug is administered, all these processes begin operating within a very short time and continue to occur concurrently. As a result, there is constant fluctuation in concentration of the drug at the site of action. Increasing the dose of the drug administered will not only increase the concentration of the drug at its site of action, there will also be a lengthening of the time that it is present in the body, as it may take much longer for the drug to be metabolized (as this may be limited by the availability of enzymes) and excreted (as this is limited by the amount of body fluids such as urine that the body can produce).

The role of individual variability on drug concentrations over time

The processes described thus far are common to everyone but there are also important differences in the way different individuals will react to drugs. Individual differences such as body weight, gender, age, health status and those due to genetic make-up will all affect the time course of a drug's presence and the intensity of its effect.

In terms of drug distribution throughout the body, the concentration of the drug in the body (and thus at the site of action) will depend upon the total volume of fluid in the body – the larger the fluid volume, the lower the concentration. In much the same way that a spoonful of sugar in a small glass of water will produce a sweeter beverage than the same amount in a large glass, a specific dose of a drug will affect individuals to varying degrees depending upon the amount of fluid in their body. For example, an average sized woman will have higher drug concentrations from a set dose of drug compared to an average man. Furthermore, women have different body compositions than men: they have on average a smaller volume of water and a higher volume of fat. The smaller proportion of water may mean a higher drug concentration at the site of action and thus a greater drug effect. We can see this most easily with alcohol where women will have higher blood alcohol concentrations following the same amount of alcohol than men of the same body weight.

Age is another important factor in determining the intensity and time course of a drug. Both the very young and the very old have a reduced ability to metabolize and excrete drugs than other people. As a result, at the same dosage, the very old and very young will have a higher concentration of the drug in the brain and it will remain there for longer periods.

Differences in our genetic make-up also play an important role. An individual's genetic make-up is expressed in protein structures and may alter drug action in multiple ways. It has been observed that certain people have highly unusual reactions to certain drugs and act as if they had used more than the actual dose they received. One impact of differences in genetic make-up is that the amount of the enzyme responsible for metabolism of certain drugs may be missing or reduced.

Thinking scientifically →
Genetics and addictive behaviours

Our genetic make-up can affect how we respond to a drug. This can occur as a result of genetically determined differences in our physiology that may mean, for example, that we are more sensitive to the positive or negative effects of a drug. Research evidence is beginning to show that genetic factors may play an important role in the risk of developing alcohol dependence. Studies that have looked at twins, comparing identical and non-identical twin pairs, have suggested that around 50 per cent of the variation in this risk is predicted by shared genetics (Brewer and Potenza, 2008; Prescott and Kendler, 1999). In simple terms, this means that a family history of alcohol dependence might give you an increased risk of developing alcohol dependence yourself. Importantly, this predisposition does not mean that genetic factors alone can cause addictive behaviours – you still need to have access to alcohol, to drink it, and to continue using over a long period of time in an increasingly abusive fashion. As such, the intention of research into heritability is not about identifying causes of dependence, rather the purpose is to identify factors that can affect the risk of it developing. A large proportion of the variation in the development of dependence disorders remains environmental.

One example is alcohol, which is metabolized first to acetaldehyde (by an enzyme called alcohol dehydrogenase) and then to acetic acid (by another enzyme called aldehyde dehydrogenase), which we excrete in urine. Acetaldehyde can cause nausea and flushing of the face and, normally, it is quickly metabolized to acetic acid for excretion in urine, and so little escapes into the circulation. However, approximately 50 per cent of people from Asia are deficient in the enzyme that metabolizes acetaldehyde (Rang et al., 2007; White, 1991). As a result, when they consume alcohol they will experience flushing of the face, nausea and heightened alcohol effects. This may stop them from drinking alcohol at high levels or at all.

So far we have discussed how drugs reach their site of action, what factors affect how much gets there, and how the body excretes the drug to end its effect. For the drugs of abuse we are most interested in, the brain is the most important site of action. It's now time to turn our attention to how a drug produces its effect in the brain and how, over time, the brain will react to the presence of a drug.

👁 Drugs and the central nervous system

The principles of neurotransmission

The brain is composed of a number of different cells; the most important for us are the nerve cells or **neurons**. Neurons are specialized cells that perform two actions: first, they receive information from other neurons; second, they pass that information on to other neurons and so continue sending the information throughout the brain.

Neurons can be thought of as being connected in much the same way as a road or a telephone line, sending information through the brain. These roads, or pathways, tend to specialize in the information that they send and the parts of the brain they traverse. For example, a part of the brain called the limbic system specializes in emotion. If we activate the limbic region in a particular way, we can feel happy. The pathway of neurons that passes through the limbic region is often called the *reward pathway*. If information travels through the reward pathway, we will feel happy and euphoric. All the drugs of abuse activate the reward pathway, and we will discuss this reward pathway in more detail below.

The information that is sent through a neuron is actually an electrical message called an **action potential**. However, neurons are not in direct contact with each other, and a small gap called a **synapse** exists between neurons. To transmit the message across a synapse, the electrical message is transformed into a chemical. Communication between neurons occurs across a synapse, via chemical means: the neurons send out chemical messengers (or neurotransmitters) that influence the activity of the next cell.

The majority of the drugs of abuse act either pre-synaptically (that is, before the synapse), to influence levels of a neurotransmitter in the synapse, or by altering the functional state of the post-synaptic receptors. In essence, **neurotransmission** is the process by which information is transferred from one neuron to another across the synapse. Figure 2.2 presents a simplified overview of this process. Drugs of dependence can affect any of these steps in the process of neurotransmission.

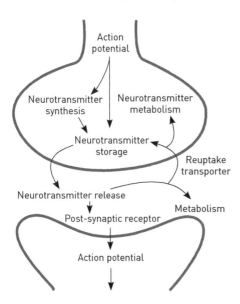

Figure 2.2 Principles of neurotransmission

As we have mentioned, the points at which adjacent cells communicate are called synapses. When a message (in the form of an action potential) arrives, the neuron will release a neurotransmitter that it has previously created and stored. When activated by an action potential, the stored neurotransmitter is released into the synapse. From there a number of things can happen: some of the neurotransmitter may bind to a receptor on the adjacent neuron and activate it, some of the neurotransmitter may be metabolized by enzymes in the synapse and excreted from the body, while some may be taken back up into the originating cell by a **transporter** molecule and be stored for another time.

To activate the adjacent cell, the neurotransmitter must attach itself to that cell, which will then initiate a biochemical mechanism for influencing the activity of that neuron. The neurotransmitters achieve this by attaching themselves to a specialized molecule called a receptor. If a receptor is activated it will then activate that cell, and by so doing, pass on the information from one neuron to another.

The chemical bonds between a neurotransmitter and its receptor are relatively weak and temporary. Many people imagine this as a process similar to a 'key and lock'. Receptors act as the lock, while the neurotransmitter acts as the key. If the correct key (neurotransmitter) attaches itself to the correct lock (receptor) then that neuron will be activated. Evolution has resulted in our brains having many different receptors each of which are designed to accommodate natural neurotransmitters. However, drugs can mimic these natural neurotransmitters and thus they can bond with the receptor, 'opening the lock'.

Some drugs will bind to the receptor and switch the neuron on (that is, it will 'open the lock' and activate the cell); we call these types of drugs **agonists**. While there is always at least one compound that acts as an agonist at a receptor (the natural neurotransmitter), there may be many drugs that can act as artificial agonists. The intensity of a drug effect is associated with the number of receptors that are occupied by the agonist and activated.

Other types of drugs will bind to the receptors, prevent agonists from binding and won't switch it on (that is, it will fit into the lock but not activate the cell). We call these types of drugs **antagonists**. Antagonists, which we can consider to be 'drug blocking' agents, are sometimes used to treat drug dependence (see Chapter 6).

The monoamines: neurotransmitters important for understanding addictive behaviour

There are many different natural neurotransmitters within our brain, and far too many to describe in detail in this chapter. However, there are three neurotransmitters that are very important to understanding the biology of drug action and addiction, and the common effects of not just drugs, but of other addictive behaviours that feel pleasurable (such as gambling). These are the **monoamines**; the neurotransmitters that operate within the brain structures associated with cognition, emotions and behaviour.

The three most important monoamine neurotransmitters for understanding addictive behaviours are *dopamine, serotonin* and *noradrenaline*. Our mood is affected by these monoamines and there is an association between altered function of these neurotransmitters in the brain and disorders such as depression and anxiety. Indeed, medical drugs that increase the amount of these neurotransmitters available in the synapse are the major medical approach to treating depression (for example Prozac and other antidepressants, which increase the amount of serotonin in the synapse).

The structures, or pathways, that are activated by these neurotransmitters commence in the brain stem and project diffusely to the cortex, which is involved in processes such as thoughts, cognition, memory and movement. Figure 2.3 provides a summary of some of the different functions associated with monoamine neurotransmitters. The monoamines are important in the control of mood and emotion, memory and thought patterns, the control of sleep, feeding behaviour and the control of body temperature. Drugs of dependence can mimic these neurotransmitters and activate the associated pathways, and many of the principle effects of drugs of dependence can be explained by this activation.

A key commonality of all drugs of dependence is that they will release dopamine in the reward pathway (see Thinking scientifically box below). Activation of this reward pathway, which traverses the limbic region, will reinforce behaviour (see Chapter 3) by producing a pleasurable response. It is likely that the reward pathway is activated in all addictive behaviours, such as gambling or eating disorders.

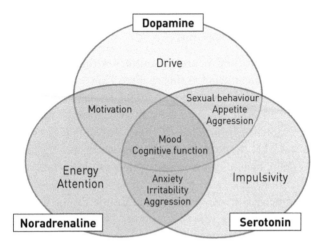

Figure 2.3 The functions associated with the monoamine neurotransmitters

---

Thinking scientifically → **The reward pathway**

Everybody engages in behaviour that is rewarding; in other words, behaviours that give us pleasant feelings. These pleasurable feelings provide positive reinforcement so that we will want to repeat the behaviour. Feeling good when we eat, drink or procreate is of course very useful for our survival.

The brain is divided into several distinct regions, each responsible for different functions. The so-called reward pathway is found in the centre of the brain and, when activated by a behaviour, or a drug, gives us feelings of pleasure and builds our motivation to repeat that behaviour. Drugs, as well as other behaviours that can become addictive (for example gambling) can directly activate the brain's reward circuitry and give us a feeling of intense pleasure.

Figure 2.4 gives a very simple picture of the reward pathway. It consists of a highway of neurons that are activated by dopamine. It begins in the ventral tegmental area (VTA), moves through the nucleus accumbens in the limbic region, and terminates in the prefrontal cortex. Behaviours such as eating, gambling, or taking a drug, cause dopamine to be released from the VTA, which then activates the reward pathway, and so affects our emotions, movement, cognition, motivation and pleasure.

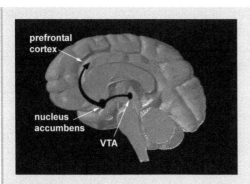

Figure 2.4 The reward pathway
This image is taken from 'The Neurobiology of Drug Addiction' teaching packet, published on the NIDA website: http://www.drugabuse.gov/pubs/ teaching/Teaching2/Teaching3.html

Thus far we have discussed what happens when we take a drug, how it travels to the brain and produces its effects upon our emotions, our thoughts and our behaviours. We now need to turn to how drug abuse and drug dependence can be explained from these biological principles.

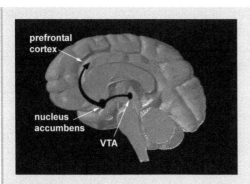 What happens after the repeated administration of a drug? Tolerance, the withdrawal syndrome and physical dependence

Drug tolerance

Our brain strives for balance and to feel 'normal'. In some respects we can conceptualize the brain as constantly adapting and changing to function in a way that we can act and feel 'normal' – a process called **homeostasis**. When we talk about homeostasis occurring in the brain we use the term *neuroadapatation*.

When we consume a drug of dependence, we alter the functioning of our brain – we upset the 'balance' so to speak. As a result our brain will adapt to minimize the effect of the drug and restore its normal function. If we use a drug frequently, then the brain will adapt to be in 'balance' while the drug is present. However, if we then stop taking the drug, our brain is no longer in balance, and it can take a relatively long period of time for the brain to 're-adapt'. In psychopharmacology we refer to these processes as tolerance and physical dependence on a drug.

When a drug is taken repeatedly (more than once), the effects of the drug will diminish each time. This is a phenomenon called *tolerance*. Tolerance can be said to have developed when a particular dose of a drug produces less of an effect. To achieve the original intensity of the drug effect, larger and larger doses will be necessary. If you have ever noticed how experienced drinkers can drink more alcohol than other, less experienced drinkers, then you have witnessed the consequences of drug tolerance.

Tolerance occurs with repeated administration to almost all the drugs of abuse. However, it does not develop to all drug *effects* with the same speed or to the same extent. Interestingly, tolerance is often developed to the more unpleasant effects (such as nausea) first. You can develop tolerance quickly to one effect, but slowly or not at all to another. For example, you may develop tolerance quite quickly to the nausea that occurs when you first inject heroin, but you will never develop tolerance to the constipation or pinpoint pupils that are also produced by heroin.

If tolerance is developed to one drug, then tolerance will also develop to all the drugs in the same drug class. For example, developing tolerance to heroin will mean that there will also be tolerance developed to all other opiates, such as morphine, codeine and methadone. This is known as **cross-tolerance** and this phenomenon can be very useful for the medical treatment of physical dependence (see Chapter 6).

Tolerance has important implications for understanding drug use and addictive behaviour. The most obvious is that the user will have to keep increasing the dose to get the same effect. For example, in the case of heroin, experienced users may need to inject heroin as many as five times a day, and will need to inject larger doses than they did originally, while a less experienced heroin user may only need to inject once or twice a day, with much smaller doses, to achieve the same effect.

Once a high level of tolerance has developed, and the individual needs to take more frequent and higher doses than initially, then it can be very difficult to come back down. Without tolerance, reducing the amount of drugs that are used and gradually stopping use altogether would be considerably easier.

The effect of a drug is determined by the amount of the drug that reaches the brain and its action on the brain when it gets there. Tolerance arises because of changes within either or both of these processes. One type of tolerance is known as **metabolic tolerance** (or **pharmacokinetic tolerance**). Over time, the speed at which the body will metabolize the drug will increase. This type of tolerance has only a small role in explaining the development of tolerance. The best example of metabolic tolerance is with alcohol. Over time, the amount of the liver enzymes that metabolize alcohol may increase, meaning that alcohol can be metabolized at a faster rate. For example, a person who drinks rarely will metabolize on average one unit of alcohol (approximately 8g of alcohol) per hour, while a heavy drinker may be able to metabolize almost twice that amount per hour (Begg, 2001; White, 1991). It is also important to note, as we have previously discussed, that continued use of alcohol would eventually lead to liver damage, which would then negate this effect in a dependent drinker.

The second and more important type of tolerance is known as **cellular tolerance** (or **pharmacodynamic tolerance**). It occurs as a consequence of changes in the number of receptors, the function of the receptors, and/or alterations to the responsiveness of post-synaptic neurons. Essentially, cellular tolerance represents the brain's attempt to seek normality by activation of homeostatic mechanisms.

Summary of the principles of drug tolerance

- Tolerance can be shown by a given dose of a drug producing less of an effect or the need for larger doses to achieve the original effect
- Tolerance can develop by several mechanisms:
  (a) The majority of tolerance is explained by cellular (pharmacodynamic) tolerance, occurring as a consequence of changes in receptor function, activation of homeostatic mechanisms, and/or alterations of neural responsiveness
  (b) The other mechanism is metabolic (pharmacokinetic) tolerance, where the rate of metabolism is accelerated with chronic drug use
- Cross-tolerance: tolerance to one drug diminishes the effect of another drug in the same class
- Tolerance develops at different rates to different drug effects
- Once developed, tolerance does *not* last indefinitely. A period of abstinence can reduce the level of tolerance to a drug

Tolerance and physical dependence are closely related, and it is the concept of physical drug dependence to which we will now turn.

The drug withdrawal syndrome

After a person has been using a drug for a long period of time, he or she may not be simply able to stop – each time the drug wears off, uncomfortable signs and symptoms will begin. As we stated at the beginning of this section, over time the brain will adapt to achieve 'balance' and feel 'normal' while the drug is present – a process known as neuroadaptation.

For people who have developed tolerance to a drug, when the effects of a drug wear off, they may start to experience a range of uncomfortable symptoms which may last from a few hours to days and possibly weeks. They may feel depressed, feel aches and pains, feel nauseous or experience flu-like symptoms. These uncomfortable signs and symptoms, representing a disruption in the physiological system, are known as the **physical withdrawal syndrome**.

A person who suffers a withdrawal syndrome when the drug is stopped, or when blood concentration of the drug drops too low, is said to be *physically dependent*. The withdrawal syndrome can be immediately reversed by administering the drug. This is an important concept as it provides a source of motivation to keep using the drug; we learn very quickly that taking the drug will stop this discomfort very quickly (see **negative reinforcement** in Chapter 3).

As we will discuss in the remainder of this book, it is possible to be physically dependent on a drug without having a compulsion to use the drug (that is, to be psychologically dependent). For example, if you were to receive morphine for pain relief after a surgical operation, you may become physically dependent on morphine and feel flu-like symptoms for a short period of time after the drug is stopped. However, you won't necessarily feel a compulsion to purchase and use morphine. Furthermore, physical dependence (that is, experiencing a withdrawal syndrome) is relatively short-lived after we become abstinent from a drug. It will generally be resolved quite quickly (depending on the drug, a period of a few days to a few weeks) after ceasing drug use. However, psychological dependence can persist for quite a long time, and many people will experience **cravings** for a drug, and subsequently relapse, well after the physical dependence has disappeared.

Withdrawal symptoms represent the unopposed consequences of neuroadaptation. That is, the balance and normality that has been achieved after the regular presence of a drug will be 'unbalanced' and dysfunctional when that drug is no longer present. As such, the signs and symptoms of the withdrawal syndrome are always the *opposite* of the effects that the drug produced. For example, if heroin were to make you feel euphoric, constipated and give you pinpoint pupils, then the withdrawal syndrome will include depression, diarrhoea, and dilated pupils.

A number of factors determine the severity of the withdrawal syndrome and the duration of time that it will be experienced. One is the *pattern of drug use*. To develop physical dependence there needs to be a sufficient amount of drug in body for a long period of time. For example, heroin produces its effects for between three and six hours. So if a person used heroin four times a day, it would always be present in the brain, and so physical dependence would develop quite quickly.

The second factor is the amount (or *dose*) of the drug consumed. The greater the amount of drug that is usually consumed, the more severe the withdrawal syndrome and the higher the degree of physical dependence. The third factor is the *length of time* that the person has been using the drug; the longer that time is, the more intense the withdrawal syndrome.

Another important factor affecting the severity of the withdrawal syndrome concerns the nature of the drug itself. Generally speaking, the longer a single dose of a drug produces an effect, then the less intense the withdrawal but the longer its duration. In psychopharmacology we refer to a drug's **half-life**, which is the amount of time it takes to eliminate half of the drug. Broadly speaking, the half-life of a drug tells us about the time it will take to eliminate (that is, metabolize and excrete) the drug, how long we will feel the effects of a drug and the time interval that we will need to take the drug again to avoid the withdrawal syndrome (Begg, 2001; White, 1991). The intensity or severity of the withdrawal syndrome is *inversely* related to the half-life of a drug. That is, the shorter the half-life, the more intense the withdrawal syndrome. The duration of the withdrawal syndrome, whether it last hours or days or weeks, is *directly* related to the half-life of the drug. That is, the shorter the half-life, the shorter the withdrawal syndrome.

These characteristics of drug tolerance and withdrawal become important when we start to discuss the medical management of drug dependence in Chapter 6. To close this chapter, let's briefly look at some of the specific drugs of dependence in relation to the concepts that we have covered in this chapter.

Summary of physical drug dependence

Most drugs that are abused are done so for their psychoactive effects. Factors common to most drugs of abuse include:

- rapid and effective delivery to the brain
- psychoactivity associated with its presence
- the release of dopamine in the reward pathway
- neuroadaptation and the development of tolerance
- the development of withdrawal symptoms after regular use of a drug is stopped

After sustained exposure to a drug, particularly when there is considerable neuroadaptation, withdrawal of that drug may produce signs and symptoms that are very uncomfortable and sometimes life-threatening.

Withdrawal syndromes are the unopposed consequence of drug-induced neuroadaptation and can persist for days to weeks after stopping a drug.

In general, these symptoms are opposite to the effects of the drug that were initially sought by the user and to which tolerance has developed.

The symptoms can be life-threatening or uncomfortable enough to produce increased motivation to take the drug.

The intensity and nature of the withdrawal syndrome is explained by the half-life of the drug:

- the shorter the half-life of a drug, the more intense the withdrawal syndrome
- the shorter the half-life of the drug, the shorter time the withdrawal syndrome will last

Physical drug dependence is characterized by tolerance to the drug and the experience of a physical withdrawal syndrome.

Psychological drug dependence can be characterized by compulsion and craving, resulting from the acute positive rewarding effects of the drugs and the consequences of tolerance and withdrawal.

◉ The biological actions and physical dependence of some of the drugs of dependence

In the final section of this chapter we will very briefly describe some of the common drugs of abuse. This section is not designed to be a comprehensive or lengthy description of the action and effects of these drugs, but more a chance to revisit some of the concepts presented in this chapter.

Nicotine

Tobacco contains thousands of chemicals, one of which is nicotine which is the drug responsible for most of the sought after effects. Nicotine can enter the blood stream by being smoked in the form of cigarettes. It can also enter the blood stream by crossing the membranes in the mouth (as is the case with pipe tobacco and cigars) or nose (as is the case for snuff). Nicotine acts on receptors, which stimulates the central nervous system and produces effects that include arousal, enhancement of mood, increased attention and reaction time, suppression of appetite and increased heart rate. Nicotine has a half-life of approximately 2–3 hours and may accumulate in the body after smoking regularly for 6–9 hours.

Tolerance develops quickly to many of the effects of nicotine, particularly the nausea, vomiting and dysphoria (that is, anxiety, depressed mood) often experienced by a novice user. In physically dependent smokers, the signs and symptoms of the withdrawal syndrome include restlessness, irritability, drowsiness, loss of sleep, confusion, impaired concentration, and weight gain. The withdrawal symptoms reach their maximum intensity 24–48 hours after the last use then gradually diminish over a few weeks.

Alcohol

Alcohol (ethanol) acts on cell membranes in the brain and is generally considered to be a central nervous system depressant (although at lower doses it may be considered a stimulant, primarily because of the loss of personal inhibitions). Ethanol is absorbed in the mouth, stomach, intestines and colon but most rapidly from the small intestine. Thus, the maximum concentration of alcohol and the duration of action are determined by the speed with which alcohol moves through the stomach to reach the intestines. After eating, solid food will remain in the stomach for a period of time and delay the movement of alcohol to the intestine. As a result, alcohol consumed on a full stomach will be absorbed more slowly than on an empty stomach. The passage of alcohol through the stomach can be facilitated by carbonation, and so champagne or mixing alcohol with carbonated drinks, such as cola or lemonade, will increase the rate of alcohol absorption.

The metabolism of alcohol occurs primarily in the liver, and humans can metabolize approximately one unit of alcohol per hour although this may be slightly increased in experienced drinkers. Metabolism involves two stages: first, ethanol is transformed into acetylaldehyde by alcohol dehydrogenase; the acetylaldehyde is then transformed into acetic acid by aldehyde dehydrogenase and this is excreted in the urine.

The effects of alcohol can be quite varied, with some people at times becoming louder and more active while others will become quiet and reflective. This is due in part to factors such as the setting in which the alcohol is consumed, and the psychological state at time of intoxication.

At low concentrations, alcohol can produce slight impairment in movement and cognitive functioning, and people can become talkative or relaxed. As the concentration of alcohol increases, people can become less cautious and more sociable, and there will be more cognitive and motor skill degradation. This will lead to sedation, increasing impairment, slurred speech, clumsiness, and marked intellectual and motor impairment until the person becomes semiconscious or unconscious. At very high concentrations, body functions will begin to break down and death may ensue. At high levels of intoxication, mood can 'switch' quite quickly from sadness, to anger, to happiness, with seemingly little reason. The relationship between blood ethanol concentration and the drug effect is highly variable, as a given concentration of ethanol will produce a larger effect when the concentration is rising than when it is steady or falling.

Alcohol has a well-defined withdrawal syndrome marked by overactivity of the central nervous system. Common symptoms include nausea, vomiting, sweating and fever and this may persist for up to 24 hours. In more severe forms, there may be tremors and seizures that are very similar to grand mal epilepsy. A condition called **delirium tremens** may develop which includes confusion, agitation and aggression. In the absence of serious medical complications, the withdrawal syndrome is usually self-limiting and in physically dependent people may resolve within several days. However, for people with a very high degree of physical dependence, the withdrawal symptoms can be life-threatening and require medical intervention.

Opioids

Opioids are a class of drugs that produce morphine-like effects. Opium is an extract of the sap from the poppy *Papaver somniferum*. This drug has been used for thousands of years for social and medicinal purposes; that is, to produce euphoria, analgesia and sleep, and to prevent cough and diarrhoea. Opioids such as morphine and codeine derive from the poppy, while heroin (diamorphine) is manufactured from either morphine or codeine by a chemical process. Other opioids such as methadone and pethidine are synthetic. They have different chemical structures to opium or morphine but will produce the same effects. For the purposes of this brief overview, we will limit our summary to heroin (diamorphine). However, many of the features of the effect of heroin, tolerance development and withdrawal are similar across all of the opioids.

Heroin (diamorphine) was developed in 1898 for primarily medical purposes. However, due to its highly reinforcing properties it soon became used for non-medicinal purposes and the abuse of heroin has now spread throughout the world. The most common route of administration is intravenous injection, although smoking (in tobacco mixture), and heating heroin to inhale the vapour (termed 'chasing the dragon') is also common.

Heroin has an elimination half-life of around 3–6 hours. It produces euphoria or pleasurable feelings and can be a potent reinforcer by interacting with the reward pathway in the brain. When a person injects heroin, the drug will travel quickly to the brain through the bloodstream. Once in the brain, the heroin is quickly metabolized to form morphine; the morphine binds to opiate receptors, which then promotes the release of dopamine within the reward pathway.

Tolerance develops to most of the pharmacological effects of heroin reasonably quickly (for example analgesia, euphoria, respiratory depression), but slowly, if at all, to other effects (for example constipation, pupil dilation). Long-term users may be able to consume up to 50-times the normal analgesic dose with relatively little respiratory depression, but with marked constipation and pupil constriction. Physical dependence to heroin and opioids can develop quite quickly. The withdrawal syndrome will commence towards the end of the drug effect (that is, approximately six hours from administration) and will reach its height approximately two days later. The first symptoms will include a strong desire for the drug (craving) and sadness. Excessive sweating, runny eyes and nose, and frequent yawning will then appear. At the peak of withdrawal people will experience chills, restlessness, body aches and pains, goose bumps, muscle twitches, vomiting and diarrhoea. The heroin withdrawal syndrome is not life-threatening but it is very unpleasant. It will generally subside within a couple of days of abstinence.

Psychostimulants: cocaine and amphetamines

Psychostimulants, or drugs that stimulate the central nervous system include caffeine, cocaine (cocaine hydrochloride), crack (cocaine base), amphetamine, methamphetamine and ecstasy (MDMA: methyl-dioxy-methamphetamine). While these drugs have different chemical structures, elimination half-lives, intensities of effect and other differences, they share many characteristics. Generally speaking, using a psychostimulant will produce symptoms that include arousal, reduced fatigue, euphoria, positive mood, accelerated heart rate, elevated blood pressure, pupil dilation, increased temperature, reduced appetite, and short-term improvement in cognitive domains including sustained attention (Cruickshank and Dyer, 2009; Cruickshank et al., 2008). At higher doses, users can become agitated, have irregular and fast heartbeats, high blood pressure and in some cases, seizures. A significant risk of high doses of psychostimulants is a form of psychosis that is largely indistinguishable from acute paranoid schizophrenia. The chemical structure of these stimulants has many similarities with the monoamine neurotransmitters of dopamine, noradrenaline and serotonin. These drugs will facilitate the release of these monoamines into the synapse, block their re-uptake from the synapse and at higher doses inhibit their metabolism.

Amphetamines are dependence-forming drugs, and dependence can be associated with adverse effects on psychiatric, health and social functioning. Chronic use of psychostimulants will lead to neuroadaptation involving fewer monoamine transporters and receptors, depletion of the stores of monoamines and neurotoxicity (Cruickshank and Dyer, 2009). The common features of the psychostimulant withdrawal syndrome are depression, anxiety and disturbed sleep patterns. While the withdrawal syndrome will generally subside within a period of a few days to a fortnight, many users of illicit psychostimulants such as cocaine or amphetamine may experience ongoing depression, anxiety, sleep disorders and other psychological disorders (Cruickshank and Dyer, 2009; Dyer and Cruickshank, 2005).

Cannabis

Extracts of the plant *Cannabis sativa* contains the substance delta-9-tetrahydrocannabinol (THC). Marijuana (or cannabis) is the name given to the dried leaves and flowers of the plant. The leaves are most often smoked or combined with food to be eaten. THC is a very lipid soluble substance, and it has an elimination half-life of several days, which is explained by the slow release of THC that has been stored in body tissues. The primary effects of THC include euphoria, relaxation, alterations of time sense, impaired motor control, depersonalization and sleepiness. Short-term memory is often impaired, coupled with feelings of confidence or crea- tivity that are not necessarily shown in actual performance. Other effects can include an irregular heartbeat (tachycardia), visual hallucinations, anxiety and panic. Tolerance will develop to many of the effects of this drug. However, the withdrawal syndrome is relatively mild and may include symptoms of nausea, diarrhoea, irritability, depression, and an increase in dreams and disturbed sleep. However, the use of cannabis may be associated with long-term psychological effects.

⊙ Chapter summary

This chapter has provided a brief overview of the biological underpin- ning of addictive behaviour. The concepts we have covered can not only go some way to understanding why people will use, abuse and become dependent upon drugs, they can also help guide us in the development of effective treatment (see Chapter 6) and prevention (see Chapters 7 and 8) strategies. We believe that understanding the biology of dependence is vital for understanding addictive behaviour but, at the end of the day, it is only part of the story. We will now turn to the psychological aspects of addictive behaviour before finally presenting a model of addictive behav- iour that incorporates the biological, psychological and social features of addictive behaviour.

⊙ Further reading

Begg, E. (2001) *Clinical Pharmacology Essentials* (2nd edn). Auckland: ADIS International.

Lowinson, J.H., Ruiz, P. and Millman, R.B. (eds) (1992) *Substance Abuse. A Comprehensive Textbook*. Baltimore: Williams & Wilkins.

Rang, H.P., Dale, M.M., Ritter, J.M. and Flower, R.J. (2007) *Rand and Dale's Pharmacology*. Philadelphia: Churchill Livingstone Elsevier.

White, J.M. (1991) *Drug Dependence*. Englewood Cliffs, NJ: Prentice Hall.

Chapter 3

Understanding addictive behaviour as a learned phenomenon

⬬ Introduction

One of the most dominant approaches to the study and treatment of addictive behaviour has conceptualized it as a process of learning. That is, addictive behaviour is something that is learned, and therefore can be unlearned. Applying the principles of human and animal learning is the basis of many useful treatments and theories of addictive behaviour, and provides us with a good way of exploring non-drug dependence.

In this chapter we will examine:
- How various learning theories have been used to understand the development of addictive behaviours
- How learning models can explain tolerance and withdrawal-like responses in the absence of actual drug use
- The importance of social learning models in understanding and treating addictive behaviours
- The clinical and practical implications of learning theories

One of the key features of addictive behaviour, discussed in Chapter 1, is that individuals engaging in addictive behaviours seem to continue doing so even when they are experiencing obvious harms. Examples of these harms are not hard to find: the Office for National Statistics (2008) reported that 3200 men and 1564 women died in 2008, with the specific cause of death listed as Alcoholic Liver Disease. In 1950, Doll and Hill demonstrated for the first time that smoking causes lung cancer. A report from the International Union Against Cancer reported that, from 1950 to 2000, some 6.3 million people had died in the UK as a result of smoking. Then, in 2003 the EU introduced regulations requiring that cigarette and tobacco packaging must display messages, covering nearly half of the entire package surface, stating, for example, 'Smoking Kills', 'Smoking causes fatal lung cancer', 'Smoking can damage the sperm and decreases fertility', or 'Smoking can cause a slow and painful death'. However, while there has been a steady decrease in smoking over the last 40 years or so, current estimates still suggest that over 20 per cent of the population of the UK smoke. That is a lot of people, being given a lot of quite worrying information, still choosing to start, and failing to quit, smoking. In another area of addictive behaviour, problem gamblers lose their homes as a result of unmanageable financial losses, directly resulting from their inability to stop gambling – a report by Downs and Woolrych (October 2009) suggested that debts of £60,000 are common among individuals with gambling problems.

Clearly the problems associated with a variety of addictive behaviours are not just severe, and indeed often life-threateningly so, but they are also often apparent to the individual and those around them. While it may of course take time for an individual to realize that their behaviour is causing them a problem, surely once an individual realizes the benefits outweigh the costs they would immediately try to change their behaviour?

Given that the harms of smoking, excessive drinking, irresponsible gambling and other forms of addictive behaviour are so obviously damaging, why do we have a problem with this kind of behaviour at all? A useful approach for understanding addictive behaviour, in terms of why it develops and why it is so hard for people to overcome, is based in behaviourist learning theory. In this chapter we will examine two perspectives on addictive behaviour, **learning theory** and **social learning theory**. Learning theories generally suggest that behaviour can be understood by examining the rewards and punishments that individuals experience during their lives, in response to the things they do. Over time, the world we live in manipulates our actions such that we will tend to engage in behaviours that get us what we want (rewards) and avoid behaviours that have negative outcomes for us (punishments). Social learning theory offers a more recent perspective on addictive behaviour, and expands upon the earlier learning theory, which tends to focus mostly on environmental causes of behaviour, to include intra-individual factors.

<⊙> Learning theory

Operant conditioning

Based on the work of B.F. Skinner (1938), **operant conditioning** is the process by which various rewards and punishments increase or decrease the likelihood of an individual repeating a particular action in the future. Rewards, or more properly 'reinforcements', can take two forms: **positive reinforcement** increases the probability of a behaviour by giving a reward, which actually means that the behaviour leads to activation of the reward pathways (see Chapter 2). So, operant conditioning begins with a behaviour that is rewarding for the individual in some way. For example, imagine that a gambler places a £400 bet on a roulette wheel in the hope that the ball will land on 11. If the gambler gets lucky and the ball lands on 11, the sizeable reward would be a £14,000 payout, plus the return of their original stake. From the perspective of operant conditioning models, this highly positive and almost immediate reward for having risked losing £400 should increase the probability of engaging in that same behaviour (that is, gambling) in future.

Reinforcement can also take the form of the removal of an unpleasant stimulus, rather than the presentation of a positive one. This is known as **negative reinforcement** – negative reinforcement increases the probability of a behaviour by removing discomfort. For example, let's say that it is raining and we are getting very wet. If we put up an umbrella we will, of course, no longer get wet. Putting up an umbrella when it is raining can be seen as a form of negative reinforcement.

The most obvious example in the addictive behaviours field is that of withdrawal – when an individual who is dependent upon nicotine decides to stop smoking, they will experience nicotine withdrawal. This might manifest itself as nausea, headaches, disturbed sleep, heightened anxiety or irritability, among other things. While the individual may wish to remain abstinent from nicotine, the fact is that the quickest way to remove these feelings is to simply smoke another cigarette. This removal of a negative state by an action is what we mean by negative reinforcement, and this can also increase the likelihood that one will engage in the behaviour again in future. In Chapter 2 we described how the withdrawal syndrome can be immediately stopped by taking the agonist. Therefore, this is an example of the negative reinforcement of an addictive behaviour.

Finally, operant conditioning can involve **punishment** – this decreases the probability of a behaviour as we will always attempt to avoid punishments. Punishment, as the name suggests, is the reason that you may avoid touching hot saucepans if you have ever been burned by one. The negative consequences of various addictive behaviours discussed previously are all examples of punishments – if you gamble more than you can afford, you will lose your house; if you drink to excess, you may vomit; if you smoke cigarettes, you will experience 'a slow and painful death'. So why, then, do people engage in these behaviours when, according to operant conditioning theory, the presence of punishments should decrease the likelihood of repeating the behaviour? To answer this question, we need to consider an important fact about the way people learn.

Imagine yourself as an inexperienced chef. You are working in a busy kitchen, and handling hot pans all day. Sadly for you, the 'Laws of The Universe and Human Biology' have been changed for the day, and as a result the nerves in your hands that detect hot and cold sensations have been retrofitted with a four-hour time delay. This means that whenever you touch a boiling hot saucepan, you won't feel any pain until four hours later. Aside from being quite inconvenient, this time lag between your action (touching the hot handle) and the punishment (feeling a very unpleasant burning sensation) also means that you will probably carry on touching hot handles for a while after, before you finally learn to avoid them (or use an oven glove). The reason for this is because people learn better when reinforcements or punishments are *contiguous* with their actions, meaning that they are closely linked in time.

Contiguity can help in understanding why it is that the seemingly strong punishments associated with various addictive behaviours often fail to stop the behaviour recurring. It takes little imagination to see that the reinforcements (the feeling of relaxation, getting 'high', alleviation of withdrawal symptoms, and so on) for most addictive behaviours are much more closely linked in time to the addictive behaviour itself than the punishments and negative consequences (health problems, breakdown of close relationships, the onset of withdrawal symptoms, and so on). In the case of our abstinent smoker who decided to have a cigarette to alleviate their withdrawal symptoms, the relief would have been almost instantaneous, whereas any punishments (for example feeling bad about not remaining abstinent) would occur later, and most definitely after the reward (or reinforcement) of relief from withdrawal.

As we discussed in Chapter 2, different routes of administration will affect how soon you feel the sought after positive effects, after taking the drug. In practice, this means that routes of administration such as injecting or inhaling a drug are more reinforcing than drugs that are taken through the oral route – simply because the behaviour (administering the drug) and the reinforcement (positive drug effect) are more contiguous.

Classical conditioning

Another important form of learning is **classical conditioning**, most often associated with the work of Ivan Pavlov – and therefore sometimes referred to as *Pavlovian conditioning*. The process of classical conditioning is important in understanding addictive behaviour because, as we shall see, it explains a wide variety of behaviours and responses among individuals who are dependent on a particular drug or behaviour.

Pavlov's classic and widely known research involved teaching dogs to salivate at the sound of a bell ringing. Now of course, most dogs do not salivate at the sound of bells ringing without good reason. Pavlov began his quest for drooling dogs by ringing a bell every time he fed them. The breakthrough discovery was that, after a period of time, Pavlov's dogs would begin to salivate merely at the sound of the bell ringing, even when no food was then given to them. This is the basis of classical conditioning – humans and animals learn to associate stimuli that frequently co-occur together (contiguously), irrespective of whether the stimuli are causally linked in any way. As a result, behaviours like salivation can end up occurring in both useful situations (like when food is being given to you – the additional saliva aids digestion), as well as not-so-useful situations (like whenever a bell is being rung). On the whole, this form of learning serves us well – it is probably quite likely in your own life that if you hear a dinner bell being rung, then dinner is about to be served (unless Pavlov is in the kitchen). However, while classical conditioning is an everyday part of the way we learn about the world, in the context of addictive behaviour, classical conditioning can work against us.

There are many things associated with addictive behaviours that can potentially come to be associated with actual engagement in the behaviour and its effects. For example, injecting drug users will learn to associate the sight of a needle with drug use, or a problem gambler might come to associate payday with going down to the local casino. In the next section, we will consider some of the implications of these sorts of association.

Thinking scientifically →
Understanding classical conditioning

No explanation of classical conditioning is complete unless it includes the technical terms. To begin with, classical conditioning starts with an *unconditioned response* (UCR) to an *unconditioned stimulus* (US). In the case of Pavlov's dogs, this was salivating (UCR) to the sight and smell of food (US). We then must find a *neutral stimulus* (NS) that does not produce the UCR – in this case, the sound of a bell, which initially does not cause the dog to salivate. The NS is then repeatedly presented with the US (ring the bell every time the dog is given food). Then, to test whether conditioning has been successful, the NS is presented without the US to see if a response is produced. When Pavlov found that his dogs were salivating to the sound of a bell, this meant he had produced a *conditioned response* (CR) to a namely *conditioned stimulus* (CS).

One of the slightly tricky things to get your head around here is the way the labels for things change, but this is worth thinking through properly. The bell starts off as an NS, because it does not produce the original UCR. Once conditioning has taken place, we call it a CS, because it is now producing a response that has been conditioned. This means that salivation can be both a UCR as well as a CR – while this seems confusing, it is important to note that salivating to the sound of a bell differs in an important way to salivating at the sight and smell of food. The reason this distinction is important is because it makes us think carefully about what behaviours actually mean – if we just ignored the causes of a person's (or dog's) behaviour, we would simply note that salivation must be happening because saliva is needed to digest food. But of course, if salivation is happening because of a ringing bell, the behaviour then has little to do with actual digestion, and everything to do with a person's (or dog's) past experience. As you will see in the section on conditioned drug responses, understanding the meaning behind behaviours can be key to changing them when they are causing harm.

- Unconditioned response (UCR): Reflex already elicited by a stimulus, such as *salivating* at the sight of food
- Unconditioned stimulus (UCS): A stimulus that can elicit the response, such as *food* which can elicit salivation
- Neutral stimulus (NS): A stimulus that does not elicit the response. For example, ringing a bell does not normally produce salivation

- Conditioned stimulus (CS): A new and neutral stimulus (NS), such as a *bell*, that when paired with UCS will produce the response (in this case, salivation). As such, the neutral stimulus becomes the conditioned stimulus after repeated pairings
- Conditioned response (CR): The new name for the UCR when the response is conditioned to the CS
- Extinction: Repeatedly presenting the CS alone until the CS ceases to elicit a response. That is, when the CS continually fails to elicit the CR

Conditioned drug responses

If a person has been using drugs consistently for a long period of time, termination of self-administration can be a long and painful process. While many succeed eventually, it is often after a number of failed attempts. Along the way there can be considerable discomfort and unhappiness. During the period of drug use, many cues in the environment (such as people, places and even emotional states and so on) have become associated with drug use, via the principles of classical conditioning. As a result, upon returning to those environments, drug cues can create craving and the urge to want to use the drug.

Typically, treatment requires a period of detoxification from the drug of dependence by decreasing doses of the drug itself or by giving a replacement drug from a similar category (see Chapter 6). This is usually followed by some sort of rehabilitation, sometimes involving counselling. After leaving treatment, the drug-free individual may report occasional unexpected episodes of a sudden compulsion to obtain the drug. In these instances, the desire may seem paradoxical – they may have many reasons to remain abstinent, but then they bump into another user, and the urge to use comes back. Such anecdotes suggest that there are involuntary factors involved, and that learning produced by repeated drug use may play a role in the mechanism of relapse.

Numerous studies have shown that one of the best predictors of successfully 'giving up' a drug occurs when the person leaves the environment in which he or she used the drug. One frequently noted example of this concerns the US soldiers returning from Vietnam (Robins, 1975). Many had used large amounts of heroin and become physically dependent during their tour of duty. However, relatively few of these soldiers continued their heroin use once back in the States. It was if they left their heroin dependence back in Vietnam. This suggests that discontinuing use of a drug is likely to be more successful if it occurs in an environment not previously associated with drug use.

There seems to be a tendency for drug use to vary according to the particular situation or environment in which the individual is placed. While biological factors involved in physical dependence are important, there are also psychological factors at play. An individual can have the same history of physical dependence and blood concentration in two different situations and be unlikely to use the drug in one, but extremely likely to do so in another. What's more, the subjective effects of a drug have been shown to vary considerably in different environments, despite equivalent dosage and blood concentrations.

Clearly, these are important phenomena. If we are to understand drug use it's necessary to know how the environment can alter the likelihood of further drug use.

👁 Studies of conditioning phenomena

When a person leaves treatment and returns to normal life, involving a number of situations previously associated with drug use, he or she may experience withdrawal symptoms – even though they are no longer physically dependent. These symptoms may make it more likely that drug use will be continued or reinstated.

One of first people to study relapse among drug users was Abraham Wickler (1948), who noted that the stories of relapse from drug users seemed to represent classically conditioned responses. He observed withdrawal-like signs in opioid users who were participating in group therapy sessions. They had been completely drug free for at least several months and thus shouldn't have had any signs of opioid withdrawal. However, when they started talking about drugs in group therapy, Wickler observed yawning, sniffing and tearing of the eyes – classic signs of opioid withdrawal. He postulated that conditioning had occurred. That is, the signs and symptoms were actually conditioned responses.

He labelled this phenomena **conditioned withdrawal**, speculating that environmental stimuli had acquired the ability, through classical conditioning, to elicit many of the signs and symptoms of pharmacological withdrawal. He further hypothesized that cues formerly associated with drug effects or drug withdrawal symptoms might play an important role in triggering relapse to drug use in the abstinent opioid user.

Categories of conditioned responses

What Wickler noticed, and many other researchers have explored, is that cues in the environment can trigger both the desire to use the drug, but also signs and symptoms of drug effects, and even the drug withdrawal syndrome. That is, these responses seemed to be learned or conditioned, and not entirely due to the direct pharmacological effect. Such conditioned responses (CRs) can be drug-like or drug-opposite depending on the circumstances. Drug-opposite CRs include conditioned withdrawal and **conditioned tolerance**. Drug-like CRs include conditioned euphoria (the **needle freaking** phenomenon) and placebo effects of drugs (under certain circumstances). We will now spend some time looking at drug-opposite CRs, conditioned withdrawal and tolerance, and drug-like CRs.

Drug-opposite CRs

Repetitive use of the same drug can produce CRs that are opposite to the direct pharmacological effects of the drug. For example, opioid injections produce elevations in skin temperature in humans, but stimuli that have repeatedly preceded opioid injections will reliably produce reductions in skin temperature when presented to experienced opioid users. This reduction in skin temperature begins before the person receives the drug. This response is as if the body is anticipating the arrival of the drug, and the effects that it will produce, and is preparing itself in order to minimize the intensity of the effect.

Drug-opposite CRs can mimic withdrawal symptoms. If they occur just before a dose is received, they subtract from the drug effect resulting in an attenuation of drug effects. That is, anticipatory response of, say, reducing body temperature when heroin is about to be administered, will reduce the absolute rise in temperature caused when the drug is actually administered. The attenuation of drug effects can also be classed as if it were a form of tolerance – and may be a partial explanation for the diminished drug effects commonly seen with repeated administration under similar circumstances of the same dose of a drug.

These CRs can produce relapse in abstinent people. In several studies, O'Brien and colleagues (1992) interviewed people who had returned to heroin use after a period of abstinence, to determine the reasons for this change in behaviour. Close to 50 per cent of people were able to identify situations that made them feel a need for the drug (craving). In such situations they experienced anxiety and illness for no apparent reason. These situations included places where drugs were bought or used, and individuals who were also present when the drug was obtained, but also included certain moods, such as feeling sad or anxious, which had previously precipitated drug use.

Conditioned withdrawal

Since in many opioid dependent people some withdrawal symptoms will occur several times per day, there may be thousands of pairings of environmental stimuli and withdrawal symptoms during life before treatment. In the laboratory, it has been shown that after as few as seven pairings between mild opioid withdrawal symptoms (UCR) and neutral stimuli (such as peppermint spray) (CS) humans begin to show signs of withdrawal (CR) when exposed to the CS alone. These CRs have been shown to be long lasting. This mechanism therefore could explain Wickler's observations concerning the onset of withdrawal symptoms when a drug-free patient returns to an environment in which withdrawal had occurred in the past.

Conditioned tolerance

Conditioned responses, which are opposed to the drug's effects, may also contribute to the development of *tolerance*. Tolerance can be described as a reduction in the magnitude of a drug's effect with repeated administration. Several mechanisms have been suggested to contribute to the development of tolerance. Conditioned drug–opposing reactions may be one such mechanism. Siegel, Hinson and Crank (1978) presented evidence that drug tolerance could be considered, in part, a classically conditioned phenomenon.

Drug-opposite conditioned responses counteract the anticipated effects of the drug. When the drug is then administered, the individual will demonstrate conditioned tolerance to the drug, as we discussed above. However, if the conditioned response is activated but no drug is administered, then the individual will demonstrate withdrawal. For example, if an individual is exposed to a heroin-related cue, this will trigger an anticipatory reaction that is opposite to the effects of heroin (for example a reduction in body temperature): unless heroin is then taken, these symptoms will feel like withdrawal. But if the drug is taken, they reduce the intensity of the effects of heroin, that is, body temperature will not increase as markedly (O'Brien et al., 1992). Siegel's studies showed that the learned aspects of tolerance follow the pattern of classically conditioned responses.

Ehrman, Ternes, O'Brien and McLellan (1992) have demonstrated classically conditioned tolerance in a group of detoxified opioid users who were studied on four separate occasions under double blind conditions. Participants received either an infusion delivered at a random interval (unsignalled infusion) of a moderate dose of an opioid (4mg, hydromorphone) or a self-injection of the same dose. On the two other occasions, participants received either an unsignalled infusion of saline or a self-injection of saline. When the opioid was given without warning by an infusion (unsignalled condition), participants showed a greater physiological response than when the same dose was expected (self-injected). Thus, the unsignalled nature of the opioid infusion prevented any warning that would bring on drug-opposite or conditioned tolerance responses. On the occasions when the opioid was expected, the conditioned drug-opposite response reduced the observed drug effects. This was supported by the saline self-injection occasion that showed greater drug-opposite responses presumably because there was no opioid in the injection to oppose the CRs. This research clearly demonstrates that simply knowing that a drug is being administered (whether or not it actually is then given) can have an effect on the way a person responds.

Conditioning clearly does not explain the entire phenomenon of tolerance, but the proportion it does may be significant. Siegel, Hinson, Krank and McCully (1982) showed that situation-specific tolerance could protect against overdose. When rats who had developed morphine dependence received a high dose in an environment different from the conditions under which they learned to expect morphine, rapid overdose signs occurred. In contrast, another group of rats with the same morphine experience showed significantly less drug effect and no deaths when given the same high dose in the environment where morphine was expected. Put simply, by removing drug-related cues, the body did not prepare itself for the various physiological effects of morphine when it was given, which had fatal consequences.

This type of tolerance may have practical implications. One is that the danger of overdose may be greater when the person is in a novel environment – one where they have not used the drug before. Tolerance may have gradually developed in the usual drug-taking situation, and to compensate for this the drug dose may have been increased. If the person then goes to a new environment they will not have the same degree of tolerance and the high dose may prove dangerous. There is some anecdotal evidence to support this. In one study Siegel and colleagues (1982) interviewed heroin overdose survivors concerning the occasion on which they took their near-fatal dose. A majority reported atypical circumstances. That is, they injected themselves in an environment where they had not administered the drug before.

The jury is still out about this environmentally specific tolerance. It's likely that relative to other factors (see pharmacokinetic and pharmacodynamic tolerance in Chapter 2), the degree of tolerance attributable to classical conditioning may be fairly small. Nonetheless, conditioning can still have a dramatic effect.

Drug-like conditioned responses

Many of the conditioned responses that have been observed in the lab have been opposed to the effect of the drug. It is suggested that what is conditioned is the body's reaction to the drug, rather than the drug effect itself. However, opposite effects are not always observed. Sometimes the conditioned response is in the same direction as the observed drug effect. One classic example is the 'needle freaking' phenomenon observed among heroin users (Levine, 1974). In situations where heroin is unavailable, some people dependent on heroin will go through the whole ritual of preparing to inject themselves, but instead of using the drug they use an inert substance (for example saline). They report a mild high, show physiological signs such as constriction of the pupils, and some reversal of withdrawal symptoms – not as good as the drug, but better than nothing.

The question of whether drug-like or drug-opposite effects will occur in any situation has yet to be completely answered. Among heroin users in treatment, the most reliable conditioned responses elicited to drug cues are withdrawal-like. Nevertheless, it is clear that experience with a drug may cause reactions in the absence of any drug effect. These reactions may be similar to (rare) or opposite to (more common) the effects of the drug and are likely to be important factors predisposing a person to further drug use (O'Brien et al., 1992). The reactions may also influence the effects of a drug taken, particularly through conditioned tolerance.

Social learning theory

The theories and research that we have discussed so far were grounded in the **behaviourist** tradition of psychological research. Behaviourists, such as J.B. Watson in the 1920s, had argued that the study of human behaviour should be restricted only to those things that we can observe – that is, psychology should be about *behaviour*. This meant that behaviourists excluded cognitive and emotional concepts such as 'desire', 'motivation' or 'beliefs' from their explanations of human behaviour. The removal of mentalistic concepts from explanations of human behaviour, and the focus on observable behaviour, was in some ways an extreme reaction to the psychodynamic psychology of Freud and others, who had flooded their theories of human behaviour with ideas of 'unconscious sexual impulses' – concepts that were very difficult to test scientifically and, in the view of psychologists like Watson, undermined psychology as a respectable scientific discipline. In more recent times, the principles of behaviourist theory are still evident in mainstream psychology, and have been incorporated into our understanding of thoughts and emotions.

Social learning theory represents an attempt to understand human behaviour in terms of both internal and external causes. *Learning theory* and behaviourism restrict our understanding of human behaviour to viewing the individual as a passive recipient of environmental influences. Social learning theory, on the other hand, endorsed a form of **reciprocal determinism** in explanations of behaviour – that is, the environment can affect us, but we can also influence our environment, and behaviour needs to be understood from this perspective. Importantly, social learning theorists such as Albert Bandura (1977) viewed learning as something that is always happening in a social context – and we need to understand how that social context influences what is learned.

Thinking scientifically →
The key principles of social learning theory

It is important to understand the key principles of social learning theory in order to see how it extends beyond the learning theories discussed previously.

1 Learning can occur via the observation of others. This is known as **modelling** or *vicarious learning*, and is a key social learning concept. Through modelling, we are able to learn about the outcomes (that is, reinforcements or punishments) of a particular

behaviour by observing another person doing it. For modelling to occur, an individual must be paying *attention* to the behaviour of another person, and they must *retain* the information in memory. In addition, an individual must both be *capable* of imitating the observed action, and have the *motivation* to do so.

2 Learning is not necessarily linked with behaviour. While this might seem like an odd statement, the point is that people can often act 'against their better judgement', meaning that our past learning does not completely determine what we will do next in any situation.

3 Reinforcements and punishments are *indirect factors* in the learning process. This view differs from the learning theory approach which suggests that learning is directly the result of reinforcement and punishment. Social learning theory suggests that these two factors simply influence the general likelihood of a behaviour recurring, or not, in future.

4 Expectation of reinforcement or punishment can be just as powerful a motivator of behaviour as actual reinforcement and punishment. For instance, a gambler who genuinely believes that they will 'win big' on their next hand in poker would, obviously, be likely to place a large bet, compared to a gambler who is convinced that they are on a 'losing streak'. In both cases, the reality of the situation (that is, you cannot ever be certain of winning a hand in poker, and there is no such thing as a 'losing streak' in a game of chance) is less important than the individual's expectations and beliefs.

Self-efficacy and addictive behaviour

Self-efficacy is a concept in social learning theory that describes the degree to which an individual feels competent or capable of performing an action. Taking the example of smoking, self-efficacy in quitting is clearly an important factor in predicting the likelihood that an individual will attempt to quit at all – if a smoker *wants* to stop smoking but feels that they are *not able* to do so, it is probable that they will avoid attempts at abstinence. Indeed, research has shown that belief in one's ability to quit smoking is one of the strongest predictors of successful abstinence (for example DiClemente, Prochaska and Gibertini, 1985).

Self-efficacy beliefs about such things as one's ability to quit smoking or drinking, or to engage in any particular behaviour, are learned through past experiences – direct experiences, as well as indirect and vicarious experiences. That is, the degree to which a smoker feels efficacious in their ability to stop smoking will be determined by many factors, including success in previous attempts and knowledge or experience of the success of other smokers when trying to quit. Marlatt, Baer and Quigley (1994) suggested that there are five forms of self-efficacy (summarized in Table 3.1) that are important in preventing and treating health risk behaviours, including addictive behaviours.

Related to the idea that self-efficacy beliefs will predict the likelihood of attempting to give up an addictive behaviour, as well as the likelihood of success, is something known as the **abstinence violation effect** (AVE) (Marlatt, 1979). The AVE is an important aspect of relapse prevention, and it describes the effects and consequences of failing to remain abstinent. Given the amount of commitment it takes to try and overcome a dependence disorder, clearly any failure to remain abstinent is going to have a negative effect on the individual. The AVE, if not properly handled, can lead to an individual catastrophizing any lapses, and experiencing extremely negative emotions as a result. It is important that individuals who are attempting to remain abstinent are given support in dealing with any slips or lapses, because they are extremely common, so that they do not undermine their own feelings of self-efficacy in their ability to keep on track (see Chapter 6 for a more detailed discussion of relapse prevention techniques in treatment settings).

Self-efficacy type	Important for:	Description
Resistance		Avoiding an addictive behaviour in the first place, for example resisting peer pressure to begin smoking or drinking. Low-resistance SE has been found to predict onset of adolescent drug use when peer pressure is also present (for example Stacy, Newcomb and Bentler, 1992).
Harm-reduction	Prevention	Reducing risks associated with use, after use, or engagement in the behaviour, has already begun. For example, beliefs about one's ability to stop or reduce drinking at any point. Interventions aimed at increasing harm-reduction SE suggest that this could help to reduce alcohol consumption among students (Baer, 1993).

Self-efficacy type	Important for:	Description
Action		Confidence in one's ability to perform the necessary actions required to achieve abstinence once an addictive behaviour has become established, which corresponds to the individual's motivation to attempt abstinence. For example if a smoker has low-action SE, they would imagine quitting would end in failure, and would therefore be less likely to try (for example Marlatt, Curry and Gordon, 1988).
Coping	Treatment and relapse prevention	The degree to which an individual will feel capable of dealing with high-risk situations during a period of abstinence, for example an abstinent smoker who used to smoke when in pubs may find they are tempted to smoke when drinking with friends, and would need to develop strategies for coping in this kind of situation to avoid lapses/relapses.
Recovery		How an individual interprets a lapse or relapse event during recovery, and their beliefs about their ability to deal with these situations. Low-recovery SE can lead to an individual feeling unequipped to deal with even minor lapses during abstinence, blaming themselves for the lapse, which can reduce the likelihood of attempting future abstinence.

Table 3.1 Types of self-efficacy (SE) which are important for the prevention and treatment of addictive behaviours

Expectancies and addictive behaviour

Expectancies have wide applicability in psychology for understanding a range of behaviours. Broadly speaking, expectancies are 'if–then' associations in long-term memory which provide individuals with information about the probable effects of their actions, based upon their past experiences. This means that we use expectancies to make predictions about our behaviour, and that our expectations are guided by what has happened as a result of our actions and observations in the past. For instance, a smoker may hold an expectation that if they stop smoking, they will experience better health and a longer life – either because they know ex-smokers who have reported better health after quitting, or because they have been provided with information from healthcare professionals explaining the benefits.

Christiansen, Smith, Roehling and Goldman (1989) have shown that expectancies can be used to predict later-life drinking problems among adolescents. In their study they found that alcohol expectancies predicted quantity and frequency of drinking, and the likelihood of problem drinking after 12 months, in a sample of 11–14 year olds. Dunn and Goldman (1996; 1998) also found that alcohol expectancies among 7–18 year olds were very similar to those held by adult drinkers and that these expectancies predicted drinking patterns among their sample.

Expectancies and self-efficacy are closely interconnected – even if the smoker in our example above genuinely believed that quitting smoking would improve their health and life expectancy, they may well avoid attempting to abstain if they also lacked the confidence in their ability to abstain (that is, if they were low in action or coping self-efficacy). It is also important to consider the importance of a particular expectancy to an individual. This is the idea of **expectancy-value** (Fishbein and Ajzen, 1975), which reinforces the social learning principle that information in memory does not consistently determine behaviour. Continuing with our smoker, who expects that abstaining from cigarettes will improve their health, let us also for a moment suppose that they are quite confident in their ability to quit smoking whenever they wish. One reason that our smoker may in fact not try to stop smoking could be because they simply do not value the outcome (improved health) of this action (quitting smoking), perhaps because they presently do not feel that they are in bad health anyway.

◉ Chapter summary

Throughout this chapter we have examined several key theories of dependence which suggest that addictive behaviours are fundamentally learned behaviours. The earlier learning theories proposed explanations of addictive behaviours that were based upon simple stimulus–response theory, excluding any role for cognitive processing. Social learning theory, on the other hand, introduced an additional layer of under-standing of addictive behaviour by including a role for the cognitive mediation of learning. While the social learning approach did not directly contradict the key ideas in learning theory, it has provided better ways of understanding the development of addictive behaviour that involves individuals and their perceptions of the world around them.

In the following two chapters we will explore more of the psychological aspects of addictive behaviour, and consider the role of mental control and choice, as well as the importance of cognitive processing and thinking skills.

⊙ Further reading

Bandura, A. (1977) *Social Learning Theory*. Englewood Cliffs, NJ: Prentice-Hall.

Goldberg, S.R. and Stolerman, I.P. (1986) *Behavioral Analysis of Drug Dependence*. Orlando: Academic Press.

Heather, N. and Greeley, J. (1990) Cue exposure in the treatment of drug dependence: the potential of a new method for preventing relapse. *Drug & Alcohol Review*, 9, 155–68.

Marlatt, G.A., Baer, J.S. and Quigley, L.A. (1994) Self-efficacy and addictive behavior. In A. Bandura (ed.), *Self-efficacy in Changing Societies*. Marbach, Germany: Johann Jacobs Foundation.

O'Brien, C., Childress, A., McLellan, A. and Ehrman, R. (1992) Classical conditioning in drug-dependent humans. *Annals of the NY Academy of Sciences*, 654, 400–15.

Siegel, S., Hinson, R., Krank, M. and McCully, J. (1982) Heroin overdose death: Contribution of drug-associated environmental cues. *Science*, 216, 436–7.

Chapter 4

Understanding addictive behaviour as a problem of control

◉ Introduction

This chapter will focus on the idea that, in some way, all behaviours are chosen by the person doing them. If we take an extreme example, such as somebody holding a gun to your head and demanding that you do something you would rather not do, it is clear that the option remains to choose *not* to do whatever is being demanded. Admittedly, your sense of self-preservation may be a very strong motivator for you to abide by your tormentor's demands, but the point is that a choice exists nonetheless – it may just be a very difficult choice to make.

In this chapter we will examine:
- What self-control is from a psychological perspective
- The importance of theories of rationality in understanding a range of human behaviours
- Theories and research which suggest that addictive behaviour is a form of impairment in the ability to exercise control

◉ Self-control

During our lives, we constantly regulate our actions – this can involve inhibiting as well as activating an appropriate response to a given situation. For example, it can take considerable effort to suppress a laugh when a friend is telling you about an extremely embarrassing, but nonetheless amusing, incident that happened to them. The outcome of your attempt to inhibit the urge to laugh could make or break your friendship. On the other hand, a 6am alarm clock in the middle of winter warns you of the importance of not being late into work – but the urge to remain in bed can, at that time, be very strong indeed. Regularly activating the 'get yourself out of bed' response can make or break your employment prospects.

Importantly, our ability to regulate our behaviour is not something that remains stable over time. Baumeister (2003) conducted a review of the research on self-regulation, and suggested that self-regulation should be thought of as a kind of mental energy or resource. The **energy model of self-regulation** states that self-regulation is a resource which can run out – this means that if you exert this energy to make yourself do something that you would rather not do, then your capacity to exercise the same kind of self-control for other activities will be temporarily depleted. People have a limited capacity to control their own behaviour, and when this capacity is exhausted, it takes time to replenish.

Muraven and Shmueli (2006) provided evidence to support the energy model of self-regulation, in the context of social drinking. In their study, they asked social drinkers to sniff either alcohol or water repeatedly for four minutes. Participants were told that they could drink the beverage if they absolutely could not resist the temptation, but that they should try not to. They were then asked to perform two unrelated self-control tasks – squeezing a hand grip for as long as they could, and another task that required participants to inhibit a response which they had previously learned to give when certain stimuli were presented. The researchers found that among those participants who reported a strong temptation to drink the alcohol, performance on both of the unrelated self-control tasks was significantly poorer. This study showed that resisting an urge to drink alcohol weakened participants' ability to exercise self-control on other, completely unrelated, tasks, supporting the idea that self-control is itself a form of energy which can be depleted.

Gailliot et al. (2007) went one step further in the study of self-control, and demonstrated our ability to exercise self-control may be linked to blood glucose levels. In their study, participants were asked to engage in various acts of self-control. Blood glucose (that is, blood sugar) levels were measured before and after, and significant reductions in blood glucose levels were noted after the tasks. Furthermore, they also found that reduced levels of blood glucose were linked with poorer performance on subsequent self-control tasks, such that participants with lower levels of glucose in their blood performed worse than others. Even more intriguingly, the impairments in self-control seen among participants with low blood glucose levels were eliminated when these participants were given a sugary drink. Odd though it may seem, 'thinking' is not in fact a free activity – when we think, we use our brain, and our brain needs energy like any other organ (Sokoloff, 1973). The harder we think, the more fuel we burn.

On the basis of this kind of research, Baumeister (2003) has argued that the development of addictive behaviour may involve a gradual reduction in one's ability to exercise self-control. Certainly, it is not hard to accept that dealing with a drug withdrawal syndrome can be very challenging, especially when one has the knowledge that drug use would alleviate the symptoms almost immediately. It then is not hard to imagine that, if a recovering drug-dependent person had expended significant mental effort trying to remain abstinent, lapses and relapses could become increasingly likely as a result.

◉ When is a choice not a choice?

While this might seem like an odd question, it is nonetheless an important one. A simple response might be that a choice is not a choice if one is forced to take it, but this is not the insight we are interested in here. Rather, this question is being used to highlight the idea that the choices we make are always subject to a number of influences, and sometimes those influences can be so strong as to make our choices seem 'chosen for us'.

To use an addictive behaviour-relevant example, alcohol withdrawal syndrome can be a particularly nasty experience and, unlike withdrawal from most other drugs of abuse, it can be fatal. So, a severely dependent drinker may one day decide to stop drinking and seek support in doing so. However, during the early stages of abstinence, they will be experiencing some potentially very aversive effects, from nausea and anxiety, to tremors, diarrhoea and insomnia. Given what we know about withdrawal from earlier chapters, we know that many of these symptoms could be alleviated by simply drinking some alcohol. This knowledge, coupled with an opportunity to consume alcohol, could and indeed does sometimes prove too much for an individual, and relapses occur.

To say that a relapsing individual has chosen to do so is in a technical sense a fair point, but it is of course necessary to consider what factors influenced the individual's decision, and indeed what might have been required to influence the person to remain abstinent and not 'give in to temptation'. The rest of this chapter will consider some of the key factors that can impact upon the choices made by those who develop dependence disorders.

◉ Personality and addictive behaviour

The study of human personality is an attempt to identify the ways in which we all differ from, and are similar to, one another. The idea of 'personality' is something that is fairly intuitive to most people, and yet is notoriously difficult to clearly define when we are asked to. In personality research, it is common to distinguish between two key types of characteristic: states and traits. Personality **states** can be thought of as transient characteristics of a person, which do not reflect the way they 'normally' are. For instance, if an ordinarily calm and quiet person is placed under an extraordinary level of stress, they may become uncharacteristically tense and irritable. Clearly, though, one would not want to use this behaviour to 'define' the person. Personality **traits**, on the other hand, are those things about a person that vary very little over time and across situations. For example, extroversion, which describes people who are confident and outgoing and enjoy being the centre of attention, is a well-researched and relatively stable personality trait.

Trait theories of personality attempt to identify those core traits that can be used to categorize individuals. The most notable of these theories have attempted to categorize the core features of personality in to 3 (Eysenck and Eysenck, 1985), 5 (Tupes and Christal, 1992) and 16 (Cattell, 1957) factor models, each listing a corresponding number of traits that were thought to be 'core' in defining personality. However, irrespective of the number of traits identified, an important question is whether there are indeed enduring and stable traits that define individuals. McCrae and Costa (1990) examined test-retest reliability of a 5-factor model over three and six years. Their results indicated good temporal stability, leading them to conclude that in most cases, personality is 'set like plaster', and other research supports the general conclusion that a limited number of personality traits change very little over long periods of time (for example Burns and Seligman, 1989).

While personality research itself might not typically be thought of as an area related to self-control, we include it here because of the interest in the field of addictive behaviours surrounding the extent to which personality might predispose an individual towards dependence. The idea that we might be in some sense predisposed towards developing dependence in many ways seems to suggest that factors outside our own control guide our behaviour.

One of the most influential personality theories is Cloninger's (1987) tri-dimensional theory of addictive behaviour. Cloninger identified three traits that predispose individuals towards substance dependence – *novelty seeking, harm avoidance* and *reward dependence*. Novelty seeking is the extent to which individuals actively try to engage in new experiences, harm avoidance includes the extent to which a person worries and is pessimistic, and reward dependence is an individual's tendency to learn quickly from rewarding behaviours, and the extent to which they will repeat rewarding behaviours in future. Variation in the extent to which individuals possess these traits can determine broad differences in behaviour, and Cloninger found that different profiles of these traits predicted different types of alcohol dependence – notably distinguishing between early- and later-life onset alcohol dependence.

Sensation seeking, a trait similar to Cloninger's novelty seeking dimension, has also been shown to predict engagement in addictive behaviours, and can be particularly important during the early stages of the development of addictive behaviours (Zuckerman, 1983). Individuals high in levels of sensation seeking tend to display behavioural disinhibition and a high susceptibility to boredom, to seek novel experiences, and enjoy adventure and thrill (Zuckerman, 1994). Given these characteristics, it is easy to appreciate why a personality dimension such as this could predispose an individual towards experimenting with drugs, which as we have seen is the necessary first step in the development of dependence (although we would reinforce here that experimentation does not always have to lead on to dependence).

Personality theories of addictive behaviour do hold a lot of intuitive appeal, and there is a lot of evidence that supports their validity in predicting differences in subtypes of dependence disorders. One of the major problems in utilizing these theories, however, is a lack of clarity on the relationship between traits and behaviour – this is a huge issue in personality theory more generally, not just in the field of addictive behaviour.

The problem can be simplistically summarized as a chicken and egg situation – that is, it is not always clear what comes first, traits that cause addictive behaviour, or addictive behaviour that causes changes in core traits. While there is evidence, some of which we discussed above, that certain traits can predict the onset of addictive behaviour, the difficulty with personality theory does not so simply resolve itself. This is because, even with evidence that a given trait (for example sensation seeking) preceded the addictive behaviour, there is no way of knowing *how* this trait led to the development of addictive behaviour, if at all.

For example, if an individual experiences a significant life event, such as the death of their spouse, then this significant stressor could lead them to use alcohol or drugs to deal with this event. The likelihood that they choose this method of coping (rather than, say, seeking support from friends and family) could potentially be mediated by certain personality traits. This would mean that particular traits could seem to be 'causing' addictive behaviour, but in fact they are only doing so in an indirect way. Alternatively, the major life event described above could potentially cause addictive behaviour directly, as well as causing changes in personality traits, which themselves could be unrelated. This is known as a third variable cause, and can lead to the mistaken conclusion that certain behaviours and personality traits are linked when they are not, purely because they are seen to occur together. Each of these alternative explanations of addictive behaviour is illustrated in Figure 4.1.

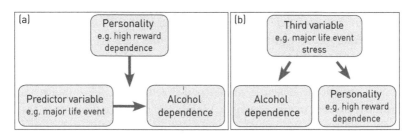

Figure 4.1 Personality explanations of addictive behaviour
(a) shows how a major life event, unrelated to personality traits, could lead to the development of alcohol dependence, but its influence is mediated by certain personality traits which could reduce or increase its influence. (b) shows how a third variable, such as a major life event, could independently affect addictive behaviour and personality, which could lead to the erroneous conclusion that the two are linked when they are not.

Aside from the apparent difficulties in understanding the nature of the causal link between personality traits and addictive behaviours, some traits are quite clearly important for our understanding of the development of addictive behaviours, even if only in a descriptive way. Furthermore, to the extent that our personalities do influence our preferences for certain behaviours and social situations, personality can be considered one factor associated with an individual's 'control' of their actions. However, what should be made clear is that while specific traits and personality characteristics are *associated* with some forms of addictive behaviour, there is no convincing evidence to support the idea of an 'Addictive Personality'. What is more important are the biological, psychological and environmental influences that develop and maintain an addictive behaviour. Anybody can develop an addictive behaviour if that behaviour serves a purpose for the individual. The view that addictive behaviours can be viewed as a rational decision made by the individual, which is consistent with their current needs and desires, has been formulated by proponents of rational choice theory.

Rational choice theory of addictive behaviour

Becker and Murphy (1988) developed a rational choice theory of addictive behaviour based on economic models of behaviour. Specifically, their theory proposed that addictive behaviours are **rational** to the extent that they are directed towards maximizing benefits for the individuals who engage in them.

Given that we understand addictive behaviour as behaviour that usually leads to, and continues in spite of, obvious negative consequences, this might seem like a counterintuitive theory. However, Becker and Murphy are conceptualizing 'benefit' in a way that differs from ordinary usage – specifically, benefit is understood as achieving one's own goals in the most efficient manner possible. Whether or not these goals are necessarily good for the individual in terms of long-term health and so on is beside the point – if your goal is to experience as much pleasure *today* as you possibly can, with no regard for the *consequences* of your actions, then it is perfectly reasonable that you might experiment with mind-altering drugs, without worrying about the longer term consequences which, we have established, are not a major concern to you.

There are a number of problems with this theory, one of the most significant of which is that the theory cannot differentiate between those who use and want to, and those who use but wish to stop (Frankfurt's 'willing and unwilling addicts' – see Chapter 1). This problem is discussed at length by Reagan (2009) who explains that, from the rational choice perspective proposed by Becker and Murphy (1988), there is no difference between these two kinds of dependent individual. Fundamentally, the theory treats them as the same, and therefore during a period of abstinence followed by relapse, the theory would also have to assume that the reasons for relapse are identical. Of course, this is evidently not the case, and everybody's circumstances and reasons for relapsing can and will be different. Rational choice theory simply does not account for this.

This problem fundamentally arises because the theory asserts that addictive behaviour is a necessarily rational behaviour – meaning that the behaviour is seen, always, as a way of achieving current goals and objectives and maximizing benefit to the individual. This is an assumption that is clearly false not only within the context of addictive behaviour, but also within the broader context of human behaviour more generally.

In defence of this theory, it could be argued that Becker and Murphy (1988) were actually trying to conceptualize addictive behaviour in a much broader sense – at the level of groups, rather than individuals. On this basis, they argued that increasing the 'costs' of addictive goods or substances should reduce consumption and use – with costs being defined broadly as any negative consequence for using, including stricter penalties for possession and taxation on things like alcohol, tobacco and gambling. While this is in principle a non-contentious suggestion when thinking about addictive behaviour as a societal problem, there is little evidence that those who have developed significant problems change their behaviour simply because of price changes, and problems may simply be shifted around society when taking this kind of approach (for example increases in criminality) (see Chapter 7 for a more detailed discussion of these issues of prevention).

Despite the problems with rational choice theory per se, there has been increasing interest in recent years in theories of addictive behaviour that view the disorder as one of choice. That is, the choices made by those who develop and maintain addictive behaviours may be guided by faulty decision-making processes (Redish, Jensen, and Johnson, 2008). We will return to this issue in the next chapter when we consider just how people make decisions, and how these decision-making systems can go wrong in the case of dependence.

Thinking scientifically →
Human rationality: How rational are we?

Rationality is a word used, more often than not, to describe a fairly positive characteristic of someone. Many of us may like to think that we are quite rational (rather than irrational), but what do we actually mean by this? It is possible to distinguish between at least two different types of rationality – Instrumental and Epistemic – and people can demonstrate greater or lesser degrees of both (Stanovich, 2009).

Instrumentally rational people are those who tend to make choices in their life that lead to them achieving their goals in the most efficient manner possible. Of course, being instrumentally rational is no mean feat – life is never so simple that we can always achieve our goals, because so many other factors affect our choices. However, the point is still a simple one: if you are an instrumentally rational person, you would tend not to make life more difficult for yourself than it needs to be. For example, if you wanted to ask a question in class, and you believed that you would be able to do so if you raised your hand, it would be instrumentally rational to raise your hand, all other things being equal.

Epistemically rational people, on the other hand, are quite another kettle of fish. Epistemic rationality is all about evaluating the contents of your mind to ensure that what we (think we) know, believe and aim for in life are all things that are consistent with the way our world is. For example, a person who is not very epistemically rational would tend to avoid listening to any information that contradicts their beliefs: even if the evidence or argument they are avoiding could conclusively disprove some belief they held, the non-epistemically rational person would rather hold on to a belief that is patently untrue than reject it and change their mind. While this may seem a silly way to behave, it is not uncommon – people tend to fill their minds with unfounded beliefs all the time, even when evidence suggests they cannot be true.

Up until now we have considered two theoretical perspectives that add to our understanding of the role of choice in addictive behaviour. However, a limitation shared by both models is the absence of any discussion of the mechanisms, psychological or otherwise, by which an individual's capacity to choose may be impaired. One model that contributes greatly towards our understanding of the ways in which choice can be limited in cases of drug dependence is incentive-sensitization theory.

⊙ Incentive-sensitization theory

Robinson and Berridge (1993) proposed their **incentive-sensitization theory** of drug craving as a way of explaining the development of compulsive drug use and urges. Specifically, this theory provides an explanation of some of the key features of many addictive behaviours, such that drug use, for example, tends to continue even when subjective pleasure has ceased (see the discussion of tolerance in Chapter 2), and that the addictive behaviour itself is often reported as the result of a compulsion to use (Miller and Gold, 1994), rather than being something the individual feels they are necessarily choosing to do.

Incentive-sensitization theory is based around the idea that the persistent use of drugs leads to alterations in the dopaminergic reward systems of the brain (see Chapter 2). These systems are involved in attributing **incentive salience** to environmental cues. In simple terms, incentive salience means that an object or cue becomes associated with a positive reward, and so is something that we will evaluate favourably in future. The neurobiological mechanism of this form of learned association is based in the reward pathways, discussed in Chapter 2. Notice also that this explanation of learning by association is very similar to the explanations of learning offered by behaviourists (see Chapter 3).

Most drugs of dependence, according to incentive-sensitization theory, hijack these reward systems, leading to a disproportionate increase in incentive-sensitization for drug-related cues, which leads to a pathological compulsion to want to use the drug. Importantly, this compulsion is not necessarily conscious, and may simply manifest a strong urge to want to use, even when the individual is aware that this behaviour is going to lead to negative consequences.

It is helpful at this point to clarify a distinction made by Robinson and Berridge (1993, 2000) between **drug wanting** and **drug liking**. The attribution of incentive salience to drug stimuli, leading to a strong urge to use the drug, is what they call *drug wanting*. Drug liking, on the other hand, involves separate neural pathways in the brain, and refers to the anticipated *hedonic effects* of drugs. For instance, using heroin because you expect that it will induce positive euphoric effects is an example of drug liking ('I use heroin because it will make me feel euphoric, and I like that feeling'); using heroin in the absence of wanting to, but feeling powerless to not use, is an example of drug wanting ('I do not want to use heroin, but I feel a strong urge to do so nonetheless').

This theory has been influential in the field of addictive behaviours, but suffered early on from a lack of evidence in humans, with the vast majority of evidence of incentive-sensitization coming from animal research (for example Fontana, Post and Pert, 1993), although in recent years more evidence has begun to emerge in human research (see Robinson and Berridge, 2008; Leyton, 2007). What the theory does clearly highlight is that use (or abuse) of drugs of dependence can lead to a 'loss of control' that is driven by unconscious motivations to use the drug. Drug wanting, by its very nature, is not something that is dependent upon an individual making a conscious decision to use. It simply reflects the learned association between the drug and positive reinforcements, and represents a form of cognitive processing that does not require our conscious awareness. We will return to this issue of unconscious processes in far greater depth in the next chapter.

While the insight provided by incentive-sensitization theory, that unconscious processing of cues drives addictive behaviours, is important, what is less clear is why many individuals with dependence disorders may be so poor at overriding these 'drug want' urges, especially when they have decided, consciously, that they want to achieve abstinence. In the final model that we will present in this chapter, we will look at how the inability to override the impulse to use is a consequence of a failure of those brain systems that are ordinarily activated in order to inhibit such responses.

◉ Inhibitory dysregulation theory

A significant difficulty with many theories of addictive behaviour is how craving and urges, and their roles in the development, maintenance and treatment of the disorder, are understood. This difficulty is compounded by the fact that 'craving' is itself a poorly defined concept, even though most people intuitively know what it means.

While craving is clearly a clinically relevant construct, it is not clear whether craving is something that causes drug use, or whether craving is simply a by-product of addictive behaviour. Incentive-sensitization theory makes it clear that drug urges may be the result of unconscious drug-wanting processes, and this theory has been a significant advance in our understanding of this phenomenon. However, one of the problems faced by the theory is that drug craving is very often not associated with use or relapse (for example Miller and Gold, 1994) – so while the theory explains craving, craving is not necessarily the most important thing to understand in the context of addictive behaviour.

Lubman, Yücel and Pantelis (2004) attempted to address this perceived shortfall of incentive-sensitization theory by developing a theory of **inhibitory dysregulation**, which takes as its starting point the notion that addictive behaviour is actually a problem of compulsive behaviour. That is to say, the central problem of addictive behaviour is conceptualized as being the apparent inability to control one's pattern of use, and that this problem is something that develops over time, starting from initial experimentation.

Specifically, Lubman et al. (2004) have presented evidence that demonstrates that while drugs of dependence may cause hypersensitivity of reward pathways, producing the incentive-sensitization effects described by Robinson and Berridge (1993), there is also impairment in the brain regions that usually allow an individual to override the impulses produced by the reward systems. These brain regions, the anterior cingulate (ACC) and the orbitofrontal cortices (OFC), are important for exercising **inhibitory control** over our behaviour, such that impairment of them would lead to behaviour that seems more disinhibited and impulsive.

Inhibitory control is particularly important in situations where an individual has to discount future rewards in order to attain some long-term goal – this becomes even more important when the individual has to suppress a previously learned response. In the context of substance dependence, a learned response might take the form of drug use when withdrawal symptoms are experienced: overriding the response of drug use, if this is something that an individual has repeatedly done in response to withdrawal over a long period of time, would require the activation of the ACC and OFC. As discussed at the beginning of this chapter, this is just the kind of effortful thinking that would involve the metabolism of, and therefore require the availability of, large amounts of blood glucose in those brain regions (Gailliot and Baumeister, 2007).

Lubman et al.'s (2004) theory of inhibitory dysregulation adds an additional level of understanding, beyond the theory provided by Robinson and Berridge (1993), demonstrating that drug dependence may lead to actual impairments in the brain regions which are required to suppress the kinds of impulsive, reward-oriented responses that typify many forms of drug use. Indeed, there is now a growing body of research that shows that the use and abuse of many drugs is neurotoxic and leads to significant damage to brain structures.

◉ Chapter summary

In this chapter we began by with a discussion around the notion of self-regulation and behavioural control, which led us to conclude that self-control requires effort in a concrete, physical sense. The rest of our discussion has focused on some key theories and theoretical perspectives that contribute towards understanding how addictive behaviour may be a disorder of control, and some of the factors that can reduce one's ability to exercise the control necessary to cease engagement in an addictive behaviour. In the chapter that follows, our focus will shift towards the concept of decision making, to try and understand how it is that individuals make their choices, and whether or not they are constrained by the kinds of influence discussed in this chapter.

◉ Further reading

Baumeister, R.F. (2003) Ego depletion and self-regulation failure: A resource model of self-control. *Alcoholism: Clinical and Experimental Research*, 27, 1–4.

Becker, G.S. and Murphy. K.M. (1988) A theory of rational addiction. *Journal of Political Economy*, 96, 675–700.

Cloninger, C.R. (1987) A systematic method for clinical description and classification of personality variants. *Archives of General Psychiatry*, 44, 573–88.

Lubman, D.I., Yücel, M. and Pantelis, C. (2004) Addiction, a condition of compulsive behaviour? Neuroimaging and neuropsychological evidence of inhibitory dysregulation. *Addiction*, 99, 1491–502.

Muraven, M. and Shmueli, D. (2006) The self-control costs of fighting the temptation to drink. *Psychology of Addictive Behaviors*, 20, 154–60.

Robinson, T.E. and Berridge, K.C. (2000) The psychology and neurobiology of addiction: An incentive-sensitization view. *Addiction*, 95, 91–117.

Chapter 5

Understanding the automaticity of addictive behaviour

◉ Introduction

The previous chapter started with the idea that any behaviour that a person engages in, including addictive behaviours, must to some extent have been 'chosen' by the individual. The theories and ideas discussed in that chapter, and indeed in the preceding chapters, give us some idea about the factors that can impair an individual's control over their own behaviour. We have seen that, while in principle choices almost always exist, these choices can sometimes be extremely difficult to make, and there are many factors that can conspire against us, which can make some choices seem almost like they are being made for us.

In this chapter we will examine:
- The role of choice and decision making in addictive behaviour
- How dual systems models of cognitive processing can be used to understand addictive behaviour
- Theories and evidence which suggest that automatic, unconscious processes are vital for understanding the development and maintenance of addictive behaviours
- The utility of this relatively new field of research in developing novel interventions

Most people are familiar with the idea of unconscious processes in the mind – even if this understanding is only based upon the idea of the sexually obsessed unconscious mind proposed by Freud. In psychody-namic theory, the unconscious is something of a slightly dark and impassioned part of our mind, full of desires and wants and conflicts. In contemporary cognitive psychology, the picture of the unconscious is far less dramatic, but no less intriguing.

It is first of all important to understand what the word unconscious means in relation to cognitive processing. An *unconscious process* is simply a cognitive process of which the individual is not *aware*. That is, consciousness is simply a feature of a cognitive process, such that a cognitive process can be *more or less* conscious. The important issue for present purposes is the extent to which consciousness is actually required for a cognitive process to happen – that is, whether or not a thought is automatic. **Automatic cognitive processes** are contrasted with **controlled cognitive processes**.

The notion that cognitive processes can be automatic or controlled is part of a more general framework in cognitive psychology that posits two distinct systems. A so-called **dual systems theory** of cognitive functioning will form the basis of our discussion of decision making in this chapter. Dual systems theory suggests that our cognitive processes are divided between two different systems, **System 1** which consists of *automatic* processes, and **System 2** which consists of *controlled* processes. Before moving on to discuss the dual systems framework, we will briefly discuss automatic and controlled processes in turn.

Dual systems theory and behaviour

For many people, the default way of understanding our own behaviour is to assume that we choose our actions, and that we 'know our own minds'. The reality of the way in which the mind works is quite different – the idea that we have privileged and unrestricted access to our cognitive processing is anything but accurate. Nisbett and Wilson (1977) dispelled this myth many years ago in a seminal article which demonstrated how often people are unable to accurately explain the reasons for their own behaviour and ways of thinking (see Thinking scientifically box below). Instead, we usually only have access to the outcomes of our cognitive processes – such as an attitude, a decision or a plan. Exactly how these outputs are generated remains hidden from view. The evidence that much of our mental activity happens 'behind the scenes' has led to a dichotomy in psychology between automatic and controlled cognitive processes.

Thinking scientifically → **Telling more than we can know**

In a now famous article in psychology, Nisbett and Wilson (1977) presented a compelling review of evidence that people are unable to provide accurate information about their own cognitive processes. This was shown to be the case, despite the contradictory evidence that, when asked, people are often quite willing to explain their own cognitive processes, and do not tend to mistrust their own explanations.

One example discussed by Nisbett and Wilson was of a study conducted by Goethals and Reckman (1973). In their study, Goethals and Reckman recruited groups of participants who had previously been asked to give their opinions on the 'busing' of students to reduce racial segregation in US schools (busing was the practice of transporting students via free buses so that they could attend schools in predominantly white or non-white areas, to reduce the prevalence of 'all white' or 'all black' schools). Participants who were either strongly pro- or anti-busing were invited to attend a group discussion with individuals who had the same attitudes as they did. Crucially, one participant in each group was actually a stooge who was sent along to argue persuasively against the views expressed within each group. After the group discussions, participants were then asked to rate their attitudes towards busing once more, and it was found that the pro-busing participants had become more anti-busing, and the anti-busing participants became more pro-busing. On the face of it, this is not a surprising conclusion – of course if you send a persuasive stooge to argue against a group, people may change their opinions. The critical finding from this study came when the researchers asked all participants to recall, as best they could, what their attitudes had been towards busing prior to the group discussion. While participants in the control group (that is, where a stooge had not been planted to contradict the group) could recall their previous attitudes with a high degree of accuracy (whether or not they had changed their minds during the discussion), the participants in the stooge-conditions actually recalled either more pro- or more anti-busing attitudes. This occurred even though the experimenters reminded these participants that they would be checking their answers with those given a week before. These participants had had their minds changed by the presence of a single dissenting voice in their group. Somewhat alarmingly, however, they did not seem to recognize that this had occurred, and even went so far as to report that they had held their current views before the group discussion had even taken place – which was demonstrably not true.

This, and many other studies reviewed by Nisbett and Wilson (1977), demonstrates the poor access that people have to the functioning of their own cognitive processes. Rather than reporting on what processes have occurred, Nisbett and Wilson showed that people tend to come up with 'best-guess' type explanations for their actions and thoughts. This may serve our own purposes in daily life quite well, but for psychologists wanting to find out how the human mind functions, relying on verbal reports from participants is clearly an unreliable path.

Automatic cognitive processing

Automatic cognitive processes, contained within System 1, are processes that occur outside of conscious awareness and cannot be examined directly by the individual. Automatic processes have been documented for a range of different behaviours, both simple and complex. For instance, Bargh, Chen and Burrows (1996) have shown that exposing participants to words relating to elderly people causes the participants to walk more slowly afterwards, and Dijksterhuis and van Knippenberg (1998) found that activating the concept of intelligence improved participants' performance in a subsequent game of Trivial Pursuit. More recently, Williams and Bargh (2008) demonstrated that participants in a study who were asked to hold a warm cup of coffee for the researcher subsequently rated the researcher as a 'warmer' person, compared to participants who were asked to hold an iced coffee. The important thing to note in these studies, as odd as they may seem, is that the participants are unaware of any link between the stimuli being manipulated by the researchers (for example temperature of the coffee) and their subsequent behaviour (for example judgements about the researcher). It is the fact that individuals in these studies respond to stimuli without realizing that they have done so which provides the strongest evidence for automatic cognitive processing.

Controlled cognitive processing

Contrasting with automatic processes are controlled cognitive processes, which are contained within System 2. Controlled processes make up the majority of what we would think of as our conscious thinking. While automatic processes tend to be rapid, environmentally triggered (for example exposing people to cues which then alter their actions) and do not involve (or at least need) conscious control and monitoring, controlled processes are very much reliant upon our investing attention and conscious monitoring to proceed. A model instance of a controlled process would be carrying out mental arithmetic. Try this example without looking at the page after you have read the instructions:

divide 576 by 9

Most people, who know how to do this kind of arithmetic without a pen and paper, or a calculator, would have gone through steps like these: How many times does 9 go in to 5? Zero times, so carry the 5 over to the 7. How many times does 9 go in to 57? 6 times, leaving a remainder of 3, which we carry across (while holding '6' in memory as the first part of our answer). How many times does 9 go in to 36? 4 times, with no remainder, so our answer is 6 and 4, 64. Printed like this, the process seems quite laborious, but with adequate concentration and knowledge of your times tables, the sum is easy and takes just a few seconds.

An important point to note here is that, rather than being an entirely controlled process, carrying out a sum like this actually involved a number of automatic processes. At the most obvious level, recognition of the value of the various figures on the page (576 and 9) was not something that you would have achieved via any effortful cognition – we simply recognize these shapes on the page as numbers, and are aware of what their relative magnitudes are. Also, while going through the process of solving the various subcomponents of the arithmetic problem, we had probably found answers like '$36 \div 9 = 4$' just appearing in our mind, without having to go through the process of '$9 + 9 + 9 + 9 = 36$, therefore $36 \div 9 = 4$'. This is because most people have learned that kind of sum by rote during their early schooling. These are automatic processes, and you will notice that they are extraordinarily useful in freeing up mental energy for concentrating on the more complex aspects of a problem.

This example serves to illustrate, then, that these two separate types of processing are in fact interdependent. In this instance, automatic processes were being used when you recognized the numbers on the page, and remembered your times tables, controlled processes were being used when you planned how best to solve the sum in your head. The way in which these processes operate and interact is the domain of dual systems theories of cognitive processing.

Dual systems theory

In dual systems theory (also sometimes called dual processing theory), a basic distinction is drawn between the automatic System 1 and the controlled System 2. System 1 represents the collection of automatic processes (of which, as we have already discussed, there are many). System 2, on the other hand, incorporates all the different types of controlled process of which we are capable. Figure 5.1 illustrates a basic architecture for a dual systems model of cognitive processing. 'Inputs' in this diagram can be taken to represent any form of information that you might process. 'Responses' can include emotional reactions, behaviours, decisions or plans. The important features of this model to recognize are that:

1 Inputs always enter via System 1.
2 System 1 is capable of producing responses in the absence of System 2 involvement.
3 System 2 is dependent upon System 1 input, so controlled responses in System 2 are also influenced by System 1.
4 System 2 processes can have a reciprocal effect on the contents of System 1.

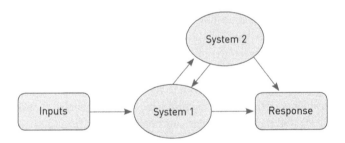

Figure 5.1 A dual systems framework for cognitive processing and behaviour

System 1 tends to try and *contextualize* information. That is, it will attempt to generalize old rules and behaviours to novel situations that may require abstract, *decontextualized* thinking. Decontextualized thinking, also known as **cognitive decoupling** (Stanovich, 2004), is the process by which people think hypothetically about the world. While this might seem like a simple idea, the power of this mental ability is massive. By being able to think in a hypothetical or decontextualized way, we are able to make predictions about the future effects of a course of action or choice, without having to actually engage in the action itself. Fundamentally, we are able to think in this way because of the existence of System 2 processes. It is quite informative to consider the range of abstract problems our evolutionarily-designed cognitive processing system has to adapt to deal with: choosing between different mortgage offers, acting as a juror in a court case, investment decisions, to name but a few (see Stanovich, 2004). Each of these decisions requires us to think in ways that are unlike anything the human species has faced in its evolutionary past (Tooby and Cosmides, 1995).

Thinking scientifically →
Deal or no deal: the cost of System 1

The game show *Deal Or No Deal* was recently described by Post, van den Assem, Baltussen and Thaler (2008) as appearing 'to be designed to be an economics experiment rather than a TV show' (p. 39). In their analysis of the behaviour of contestants across the various countries in which the show is broadcast, Post et al. (2008) demonstrated what any objective viewer would be able to attest to: contestants hardly ever seem to make the most sensible decision based on the balance of probabilities and expected losses or gains. It is not uncommon for contestants on the show to use a 'system' to select boxes, or to remark that they have a good or bad 'feeling' for the box they have selected or brought to the table with them.

This is a good example of contextualized thinking working against people – when someone takes a huge financial risk on the basis that their box number relates to an important date (the birth of their son, or the year of their wedding), they are letting completely irrelevant information influence their judgements.

The box above describes an example, involving probabilistic decision making, which highlights how System 1 processing can work against us. This is due to the adaptive, albeit not always appropriate, tendency of System 1 to streamline cognitive processing as far as possible – fundamentally we are **cognitive misers**, meaning that we tend to avoid effortful (System 2) thinking whenever possible. As a result, individuals must often override many of the outputs of System 1 when the present situation demands it, but this can be difficult at the best of times. The Thinking scientifically box below describes an example of just how influential this tendency of System 1 to look for **heuristics** and shortcuts in our thinking can be, even when we are under the impression that we are in fact using controlled System 2 processes.

Thinking scientifically → **System 1 is efficient, and System 2 is adaptable ... but which is better?**

There are obvious benefits to having both System 1 and System 2 cognitive processes, but do they always work in harmony? Stanovich (2004) uses an example of **syllogistic reasoning** to illustrate this point. Read the following two sets of statements, and decide whether the final line in each would *have to be true* if the first two premises were true. If the two premises guarantee the conclusion being true, then the syllogism is said to be valid.

Syllogism 1

Premise 1: All living things need water

Premise 2: Roses need water

Therefore, Roses are living things

Syllogism 2

Premise 1: All insects need oxygen

Premise 2: Mice need oxygen

Therefore, Mice are insects

Have you made your decision? Okay then: upon careful consideration, it is quite obvious that syllogism 1 is false. That is, the first two statements, even though we know they are true, do not guarantee that the conclusion is true, even though we know that it is actually true also (NB the same is also true for syllogism 2, although we also just happen to know that the conclusion is definitely false). Here is why: premise 1 tells us that all things that are living need water, which is not the same as saying that all things that need water are living things. So, when we are told that a rose needs water, we are not correct in assuming that it is necessarily a living thing. However, because of the prior knowledge we have that roses are indeed living things, around 70 per cent of people encountering this problem proclaim the syllogism to be logically valid.

What does this tell us about Systems 1 and 2? Having understood the explanation above, you will have been using System 2 to work through the arguments presented – it takes a bit of effortful, focused thinking to get your head around the logic. If you, like 70 per cent of people given this task, said that Syllogism 1 was valid, this demonstrates that you were using prior knowledge (about roses needing water *and* being living things) to quickly answer a question which actually required you to think a little more carefully (that is, to use System 2).

On reading the first syllogism, it probably just 'felt right', and you used this mental shortcut or heuristic to obtain an answer which you thought was correct. On the other hand, syllogism 2 'feels' wrong because we already know that mice are not insects. So even though most people get syllogism 2 correct, it is not usually because they actually thought through the logic of it (be honest – did you?).

Dual systems models of human thinking have been present, in one form or another, in psychology for almost as long as the discipline has existed (see Schneider and Chein, 2003, for a review of this area) and in recent years have increasingly been applied to the understanding of a variety of phenomena, such as the effects of alcohol on behaviour (Moss and Albery, 2009; Wiers and Stacy, 2010; Moss and Albery, 2010); health-risk decision making (Gerrard et al., 2008); and depression (Beevers, 2005; Andrews and Thomson, 2009). Many of the shortcomings of the automatic System 1 only become apparent in the context of some of the 'unnatural' demands placed upon individuals living in modern societies. In many, if not most, other instances, System 1 quietly and efficiently guides us through our daily lives without causing problems. The case of addictive behaviour, unfortunately, is one where the defaults of our cognitive processing systems can fail to protect us from harm, with evidence for deficits in reasoning from a dual systems perspective providing insights into the nature of the problems underlying addictive behaviour (see Redish, Jensen and Johnson, 2008). In Chapter 8 we will present a new model that builds upon the dual systems perspective by showing how it links with other biological, psychological and social factors, but for the remainder of this chapter we will consider the evidence that supports the utility of this framework for understanding addictive behaviours.

Dual systems theory and addictive behaviour

Tiffany's craving model

In the previous chapter we discussed the theory of incentive-sensitization which suggested that drug urges and craving may be the result of sensi-tivities which develop in the brain's reward systems, and which become hyperactive when drug users are exposed to drug-related stimuli. This theory introduced an important idea, which we promised to return to in this chapter, that drug urges could potentially operate unconsciously. In the context of Robinson and Berridge's (1993) theory, unconscious urges are called *drug wanting*, and this drug wanting does not necessarily relate to any expectation of pleasure from drug use (which they call *drug liking*). Drug wanting is literally the activation of the reward system which generates a compulsion to 'want' to use the drug, even if the individual has a longer term goal to abstain.

In this chapter we are exploring in more detail the nature and function of unconscious and automatic processes, and their relation to addictive behaviour. Tiffany (1990; 1999) developed a model of drug craving which attempts to explain why craving occurs, and how it is related to future use, using a dual systems framework of automatic and controlled processing mechanisms.

Tiffany argued that dependence is a form of automatic behaviour, and that continued use of drugs over time leads to the development of automatic *drug-use representations* in memory. Drug-use representations are simply the knowledge or mental **schema**, stored in memory, which relate to an individual's ability to use drugs – for instance, knowledge of how to inject oneself with heroin, how to roll a cigarette, or how to obtain a drug from a known source. In saying that this information becomes automatic, we are essentially saying that the behaviour has become habitual and can be performed without much mental effort (compare this with the kind of concentration that a novice smoker would require in the act of rolling their first ever cigarette).

Tiffany (1990) suggested that the development of addictive behaviours is comparable to learning how to drive a car – the behaviour begins as something that requires effortful thought to perform as we need to learn how to operate the gear shift, how the car responds to pressure applied on the accelerator pedal, and so on. Over time what was once so difficult to learn becomes automatic or 'habitual', and we can drive a car with what feels like minimal effort, and direct more of our attention to what is happening on the road in front of us. In much the same way, Tiffany's model suggests that addictive behaviours become more 'effortless' and habitual over time.

In a way that is reminiscent of Robinson and Berridge's (1993) distinction between drug liking and drug wanting, Tiffany argued that craving has two components – an automatic and a controlled component. Automatic craving involves the activation of drug-use representations or schemata in memory, which would lead to drug use. This kind of craving does not necessarily have to be conscious, and may be experienced by the individual as a fairly unremarkable compulsion to use. Controlled craving, on the other hand, is the kind of craving that most people immediately think of when they hear the word 'craving' – an intense feeling of wanting and needing something, often accompanied by negative emotional reactions when the focus of our desire is beyond our reach. Tiffany's explanation for the difference between these two types of craving is that controlled craving only occurs when an obstacle prevents the aims of the automatic process from being achieved (for example, having no access to alcohol would interrupt an automatic 'drink alcohol' schema, and lead to craving). The implication of this is that, when there is no obstacle, drug use is something that can happen entirely automatically – or as Ludwig (1988) puts it in the context of alcohol dependence: 'Others [problem drinkers] essentially think instinctively, short circuiting both imagery and cognitions, and are inclined to act without knowing why. When alcohol becomes readily available, they drink before they think.' When the automatic drug-use representation is not able to seamlessly achieve its outcome, Tiffany's model suggests that controlled processes are engaged, via the subjective and aversive feeling of craving, to compel the individual to overcome this obstacle and achieve the original goal (that is, to use the drug).

The idea that craving is the result of a failure of automatic processes to achieve their aims (that is, to engage in the addictive behaviour) is an important one – it leads to the intuition, supported by Tiffany's research, that information related to addictive behaviour, including schemata and representations in memory related to actual use or engagement in the behaviour, become active and guide behaviour without the need for conscious control or monitoring. Furthermore, these schemata will become stronger with time, as the individual gains more and more experience of engaging in the behaviour – quite literally, the representations in memory become stronger and more easily activated. Once active, they will cause you to become hypersensitive towards anything related to the addictive behaviour, and you just cannot get it out of your mind. The next section will describe how our conscious attention becomes hijacked, and how this hijacking can increase the likelihood of engaging in addictive behaviour.

Attentional biases and addictive behaviour

People tend to notice and pay attention to the things that matter to them, and this phenomenon is known as **attentional bias**. A significant amount of research in the area of drug and alcohol use has shown attentional biases among both problem and non-problem users of a variety of different substances.

A recent review of one attentional bias measure, the *modified Stroop test* (see Thinking scientifically box below), revealed that attentional biases for alcohol-related cues seem to increase as a function of past use

(Cox, Fadardi and Pothos, 2006). Other authors have suggested that this increase follows 'a graded continuity of attentional bias underpinning the length of the consumption continuum' (Jones, Bruce, Livingstone and Reed, 2006, p. 171).

Weinstein and Cox (2006) argued that attentional biases are an important component in the process of drug-seeking, and the eventual development of addictive behaviour. Their review provided an integrative framework for drug use, which suggested that attentional biases increase the motivation to seek out and use drugs/alcohol – and that drug-use behaviour in itself produces increased vigilance for drug cues.

More recently, Field and Cox (2008) developed a theoretical model proposing that substance-related stimuli come to elicit expectations of substance availability through classical conditioning. These expectancies create an attentional bias for drug/alcohol-related stimuli as well as increasing subjective craving. In addition, a recent meta-analysis has indicated a weak but significant relationship between attentional bias and craving across a number of addictive disorders, using a number of attentional bias measures (Field, Munafo and Franken, 2009).

Thinking scientifically → **Measuring attentional bias**

The classic Stroop task (Stroop, 1935) is an excellent demonstration of how certain abilities become so automatic that individuals are incapable of stopping them. In the classic Stroop, participants are shown colour-words (red, green, yellow, blue), and each word is written in either a congruent colour (that is, the word red written in red ink) or an incongruent colour (that is, the word red written in blue, yellow or green ink). Participants are simply asked to ignore the words and report the ink colour. On congruent trials, people find it very easy to respond quickly, because the word and the ink colour match up. However, it is very difficult to respond quickly and accurately in the incongruent conditions – this is because, try as we might, it is nearly impossible to stop oneself reading a familiar word, and this interferes with correctly responding on the Stroop task.

The Stroop task has been modified for measuring attentional bias in drug and alcohol research, using words that relate to, for example, alcohol, and some other neutral category of words. The task works in a similar way to the classic Stroop, and attentional biases are identified when participants take longer to respond to the colour of alcohol-related words compared to neutral words. This slowing down when trying to state the colour of alcohol words indicates that an individual is distracted by the word, because it means something to them.

The assumption that attentional biases are directly associated with ongoing addictive behaviour has led to the development of interventions aimed at reducing or eliminating substance-related attentional bias. Recent research has found that attentional retraining for alcohol- and smoking-related stimuli did lead to reductions in attentional bias, but these effects did not generalize beyond the training task used, nor were any changes related to participants' use or craving (Schoenmakers et al., 2007; Field et al., 2007; Field, Duka, Tyler and Schoenmakers, 2009). Fadardi and Cox (2009) reported that reductions in attentional bias, achieved using a complex intervention incorporating attentional retraining, were effective in reducing attentional bias and produced modest but significant reductions in drinking behaviour in a sample of heavy non-dependent drinkers. To date, there has been only one study (Schoenmakers et al., 2010) showing that attentional retraining may be effective as an intervention among dependent drinkers, but given the complex nature of dependence disorders, one would not expect an intervention like this to be effective unless incorporated into a broader programme of care (see Chapter 6 for a fuller discussion of integrated treatment programmes).

Franken's model of drug craving and addictive behaviour

Franken (2003) has attempted to integrate evidence from attentional bias research with a wide range of other evidence to explain craving and relapse. The model has provided convincing neurological and pharmacological evidence to explain the mechanism of attentional bias, and its role in drug craving and relapse. Similarly to both the incentive-sensitization theory and Tiffany's (1990) craving model, Franken suggests that the perception of drug-related stimuli leads to increased dopaminergic activity in the reward pathway of dependent users. This increase in dopamine release is hypothesized by Franken to be the driver of attentional bias towards these stimuli, which in itself can lead to drug craving as attention is increasingly directed towards drug-related stimuli.

The implication of this so-called hypervigilance for drug stimuli is that attentional resources become overwhelmed, to the point that an individual will be left with no attentional resources to attend to other information. This could leave an individual incapable of processing information related to, for example, coping with intense feelings of craving or compulsions to use. In this situation, lapses and relapse would become increasingly likely to occur, as behaviour would be expected to become increasingly guided by System 1, automatic processing. If we also consider Lubman, Yücel and Pantelis's (2004) work, discussed in the previous chapter, on inhibitory dysregulation, which suggests that neurotoxicity in the orbital frontal cortex reduces an individual's ability to inhibit impulsive urges to use, a fuller picture begins to develop of the extent to which dependence disorders systematically reduce an individual's capacity to exert 'self-control'. In Chapter 8 we will build upon these models.

Two systems, one person: System 1 and 2 interactions in addictive behaviour

A recent and fascinating line of research has begun to demonstrate that drug-use behaviours are the result of complex interactions between activity that occurs within both Systems 1 and 2. In one study, Houben and Wiers (2009) took measures of both System 1 (automatic positive associations with alcohol) processing and System 2 (ability to inhibit responses). Their results demonstrated that positive associations with alcohol were related to alcohol consumption, but only among those participants who scored poorly on the response-inhibition task. Among participants who scored highly in their ability to inhibit responses, automatic positive alcohol associations were unrelated to drinking behaviour.

Other similar research is beginning to support the idea that drug- and alcohol-related behaviours can be more completely understood, explained and even predicted when consideration is given to both automatic and controlled cognitive processes (Wiers, Beckers, Houben and Hofmann, 2009; Friese, Bargas-Avila, Hofmann and Wiers, 2010). Specifically, the important message seems to be that if an individual has learned negative health risk behaviours, and these behaviours have become automatic, then it is necessary for the individual to be able to exert controlled processing (that is, to engage System 2 resources) to overcome the urges to engage in these behaviours. The evidence that we have discussed throughout this and the preceding chapters, however, seems to indicate that it is this capacity that can become weakened as a result of continued drug use.

It is also well established that many drugs of dependence, including alcohol, selectively impair controlled processing ability in acute situations of use. That is, when an individual consumes alcohol, for example, controlled processing is weakened as a function of the amount of alcohol they have consumed, whereas automatic processing capacity seems to be almost unaffected (Moss and Albery, 2009). This means that the individual's behaviour is far more likely to be guided by previously learned patterns of behaviour, so if they have consumed alcohol in a very hazardous way in the past, the likelihood that this behaviour will happen again increases each time they have another drink. One reason why hazardous drinking behaviours may be so persistent, even among those who are not dependent on alcohol, is that the negative consequences are hardly at all contiguous with the behaviour. Positive consequences (for example increased sociability, relaxation), on the other hand, are immediately apparent.

The importance of this area of research is that it demonstrates that a complete understanding of any behaviour cannot be restricted to a study of either system in isolation – while System 1 is viewed as the default system for cognitive processing, it can be overridden by System 2, providing System 2 is intact, and the individual possesses both the motivation to, and knowledge of how, to engage this system to guide their behaviour for their own benefit.

The case of problem gambling: when your mind lacks software

In the majority of the research and theories discussed in this chapter, there has been a clear bias towards alcohol and other drugs. However, many of the concepts and ideas that we have discussed can easily be applied to other forms of addictive behaviour, such as problem gambling. Gambling is an especially interesting topic in the current context, because the gambling industry is particularly adept at exploiting many of the biases in reasoning which we discussed earlier in this chapter.

Fruit machines are an excellent example – have you ever noticed how, if you lose money on a fruit machine, it stays eerily silent, but if you win, you get lots of congratulatory flashing lights and the heart-warming chink of coins hitting the collection tray? Think this through: basic behaviourist theory (Chapter 3) tells us that this is an excellent way of setting up a fruit machine if you want to encourage continued play – whereas some kind of embarrassing, attention-grabbing fanfare might act as a form of punishment when the player has missed the jackpot, and therefore discourage future play. From a cognitive perspective, which events do you think a player will be more likely to recall: the very few times when they won the £50 jackpot, to the sound of 50 individual 'clinks' of each coin falling, or the many nondescript, non-memorable occasions on which money was lost with no payout?

Gambling is also interesting because, even for non-problem gamblers, the maths involved is not always that easy to calculate, and for a variety of reasons people generally tend to hold odd views about probabilities and find it difficult to understand information about risk when it is presented in probabilistic form (Visschers, Meertens, Passchier and De Vries, 2009).

Toplak et al. (2007) investigated the specific biases in thinking among dependent gamblers, and identified three specific failures in reasoning that were associated with their dependence:

- *Overriding System 1 processes:* problem gamblers in their study found it particularly difficult to inhibit the automatic responses of System 1, even in situations where they may have determined that the System 1 response is not optimal.
- *Incomplete System 1 outputs:* this refers specifically to emotional outputs, which emerge from System 1. Toplak et al. (2007) explain that it can sometimes be the case that an individual fails to experience, or be able to express, their emotional reactions to a situation. Problem gamblers in their study tended to have difficulties identifying and describing their emotions.
- *Missing mental software:* while it is obvious that optimal strategies in gambling (or indeed any other behaviour) require an individual to have the mental tools to be able to solve a particular problem, it is sometimes the case that an individual simply does not possess sufficient knowledge to solve a particular problem, or the knowledge they have may be false. In the context of the problem gamblers, this manifested itself as an increased likelihood of holding erroneous beliefs about probabilities and relative risks in gambling situations.

This research provides an interesting insight into the ways in which psychological dependence can develop when individuals are predisposed towards these behaviours because of deficits in their thinking skills. Something as simple as having a false understanding of the risks involved in gambling could well be the first step towards risky engagement in the behaviour. Indeed, as we will see in Chapter 6, many of the psychosocial interventions for dependence disorders involve helping individuals to understand their cognitive processes, and how these may be working against the individual to maintain the addictive behaviour that they are struggling to overcome.

⟨⊙⟩ Chapter summary

In this chapter we have covered a large amount of complex material relating to basic cognitive psychological research, and cutting edge work that is ongoing in the field of addictive behaviour. However, while much of the work discussed is in its infancy, compared to most other fields of research in the addictive behaviours, it is hopefully apparent that there is much to be gained from a dual systems framework in terms of both our understanding of addictive behaviour, and the development of new interventions to prevent and minimize harms among dependent users.

In the following two chapters we will discuss in greater depth the available treatments and interventions for dependence disorders (Chapter 6), as well as strategies that are aimed at preventing addictive behaviour from developing in the first place (Chapter 7). Our final chapter will be spent drawing together the disparate theoretical ideas presented in this book.

⟨⊙⟩ Further reading

Field, M. and Cox, W.M. (2008) Attentional bias in addictive behaviors: A review of its development, causes and consequences. *Drug and Alcohol Dependence*, 97, 1–20.

Franken, I.H.A. (2003) Drug craving and addiction: Integrating psychological and neuropsychopharmacological approaches. *Progress in Neuro-Psychopharmacology and Biological Psychiatry*, 27, 563–79.

Houben, K. and Wiers, R.W. (2009) Response inhibition moderates the relationship between implicit associations and drinking behavior. *Alcoholism, Clinical and Experimental Research*, 33, 626–33.

Moss, A.C. and Albery, I.P. (2009) A dual-process model of the alcohol–behavior link for social drinking. *Psychological Bulletin*, 135, 516–30.

Nisbett, R. and Wilson, T. (1977) Telling more than we can know: Verbal reports on mental processes. *Psychological Review*, 84, 231–59.

Schoenmakers, T.M., deBruin, M., Lux, I.F.M., Goertz, A.G., Van Kerkhof, D.H.A.T. and Wiers, R.W. (2010). Clinical effectiveness of attentional bias modification training in abstinent alcoholic patients. *Drug and Alcohol Dependence*, 109, 30–6

Stanovich, K.E. (2004) *The Robot's Rebellion: Finding Meaning in the Age of Darwin*. Chicago: University of Chicago Press.

Tiffany, S.T. (1990) A cognitive model of drug urges and drug-use behavior: Role of automatic and nonautomatic processes. *Psychological Review*, 97, 147–68.

Toplak, M.E., Liu, E., Macpherson, R., Toneatto, T. and Stanovich, K.E. (2007) The reasoning skills and thinking dispositions of problem gamblers: A dual-process taxonomy. *Journal of Behavioral Decision Making*, 20, 103–24.

Chapter 6

Treatment options for addictive behaviours

👁 Introduction

In this chapter we will be turning our attention to some of the treatment options available to help those who have developed an addictive behaviour. While most people will attempt to deal with their addictive behaviour by themselves, and indeed many will be eventually successful, there are those who may find that they need some additional support. For some, the addictive behaviour may have led to serious health, legal, social or other problems that will require professional assistance.

In this chapter we will examine:
- The process of drug dependence treatment
- Pharmacological and medical approaches to the treatment of addictive behaviours
- Psychosocial approaches to the treatment of addictive behaviours
- Evidence for the effectiveness of these treatment approaches

Often those who seek treatment for drug dependence have developed significant tolerance to the positive effects of the drug, with the majority of continued drug use being to avoid uncomfortable withdrawal symptoms. As we described in the first chapter, an addictive behaviour often involves the person spending more and more time on obtaining a drug, or recovering from its effects, and less and less time spent on other activities such as doing a good job at work, keeping relationships going and so forth. We also discussed how this can lead to serious health, legal (especially if an illicit drug is consumed), employment, relationship and other problems. Often the decision to enter treatment is made in this context and many people will seek treatment when they feel that they have hit 'rock bottom'; that is, when the problems associated with their addictive behaviour become overwhelming.

Stopping an addictive behaviour can be a very difficult and long process, and often multiple attempts at treatment are required before success is finally achieved. For those with serious medical, psychological and social problems, the first priority may be to minimize the harms associated with the addictive behaviour before the drug or other dependence is tackled directly. This combination of physical, psychological and psychosocial dimensions makes drug dependence a difficult condition to treat. To be successful, we need to address all these dimensions and any associated health problems, and as a result, treatment may take a long time.

While treatment for drug dependence may not always ensure that every individual will achieve a state of abstinence and never relapse, there is no doubt that drug dependence treatment is a vital service. There is a large body of scientific evidence to show that drug dependence treatment is effective in improving health, legal and psychosocial status and in reducing the costs associated with other health and social services. It has been estimated that for every £1.00 spent on providing treatment, there is a £2.50 saving to the community in terms of reduced costs of policing, and health and social welfare services (Davies et al., 2009).

There are many different types of treatments and many different theoretical approaches underpinning these different treatment approaches. Many treatment programmes will combine elements from the different approaches, while others adopt a single approach. The essential key to achieving success in treatment is to find the best match for the individual. It may be necessary to try a variety of different approaches before the approach that best suits is found.

This chapter will provide a brief overview of some of the more important pharmacological (that is, medical) and psychosocial treatment approaches that are in current use. Each of these different approaches is built upon the basic elements of addictive behaviour that we have discussed in this book. The focus of this chapter will be upon the treatment of alcohol and other drug dependence; however, many of the elements covered can also be applied to other addictive behaviours.

⊙ An overview of the process of drug dependence treatment

Before describing some of the treatment approaches available, let's start by describing the broad categories of treatment and the general process of providing treatment.

Many drug users will be reluctant to enter treatment, especially if they are in the precontemplation stage of change (see Chapter 1). There are significant health and psychosocial harms associated with drug dependence, indeed with any addictive behaviour. For some people it is frequently a crisis, such as financial or legal problems, that triggers a desire to receive treatment. As such, it is important to be able to engage with these people quickly, to take advantage of this increased motivation.

No matter what stage of change the person is in, the first step in reducing the harms to the individual and to the broader society associated with drug dependence is to make contact with the individual. The first category of treatment, which we can describe as *making contact with drug users*, is designed to provide factual information about drug use, assist in the safer use of drugs to minimize harms and facilitate access to the available treatment options (Gowing, Proudfoot, Henry-Edwards and Teeson, 2001). For some, receiving information about drugs and their associated harms can help a person move from the precontemplation stage to higher stages of change such as contemplation or action. This group of treatment strategies includes peer outreach services, clean needle and syringe exchange programmes, primary health providers (such as GPs, nurses and other health workers), social welfare workers, police and so forth.

The second category of treatment is focused more directly on assisting a person cease drug taking than on the information and general health strategies (Gowing et al., 2001). As we discussed in Chapter 2, drug dependence can involve a physical adaptation to chronic drug use and the development of uncomfortable or life-threatening withdrawal symptoms when drug use is stopped. The second category of drug treatment is called **detoxification**, and it is designed to help the person deal with the uncomfortable or harmful symptoms during the withdrawal syndrome to ensure that it is completed safely and comfortably.

The withdrawal syndrome is often a factor in relapse to drug use, as the person will learn that by taking the drug the symptoms will cease immediately (see Chapters 2 and 3). As a result, the alleviation of withdrawal symptoms with prescribed medication may help to avert relapse in the short term. For some people, additional medical treatment may also be required for potentially life-threatening complications associated with drug dependence and withdrawal (such as seizures, psychoses and so forth).

Many drug-dependent people may be able to stop taking drugs without such medical or other assistance, but for some people it is vital. Detoxification is not considered a treatment for drug dependence in its own right, as it is designed to assist only with the management of physical dependence (that is, withdrawal syndrome) rather than the broader aspects of psychological dependence and craving for the drug (Melmon, Morrelli, Hoffman and Nierenberg, 1992; White, 1991). Indeed, there is a very high rate of relapse among people who have completed a detoxification programme (Gowing et al., 1991). Nonetheless, it is an important service and can help attract the person into more comprehensive forms of treatment.

The third category of treatment involves the medical and pharmacological treatment of drug dependence and is called *drug substitution treatment*. This approach involves the prescription of a drug with a similar action to the drug of dependence but with a lower degree of risk. For example, for those attempting to stop smoking, nicotine patches and gum will provide the drug but without the harmful constituents of the smoke. Other examples include the use of a long-acting opioid called methadone with people who are dependent upon heroin, and the use of a medical stimulant such as amphetamine with those who are dependent upon illicit stimulants such as methamphetamine (also known as 'crystal meth' or 'ice'). However, this approach is not available for all drugs. For example, the harms associated with alcohol dependence are due to the alcohol itself, not a contaminant or the means of administration, and so substitution with a safer form of alcohol is currently not possible.

The value of substitution treatment is that it will stabilize the physical condition of the user by alleviating the withdrawal syndrome, removing the need to obtain the drug. By so doing, the person has the opportunity to focus upon other aspects of health and psychosocial functioning and to help develop a new drug-free lifestyle and social network. Often substitution treatment is provided over a long period of time and participants receive additional forms of treatment to assist with the eventual move to a drug-free lifestyle (Gowing et al., 2001; Rang et al., 2007; White, 1991).

The fourth category of treatment involves the use of *blocking* or *aversive drugs*. Psychological conditioning has a large role to play in the initiation and continuation of drug use; the euphoric and sought after effects of drugs can be powerful positive reinforcers (see Chapter 3). The rationale of blocking and aversive agents is to remove the positive reinforcement of drug use. This form of treatment will be offered once an individual has successfully been detoxified from a drug (that is, no longer experiencing the drug withdrawal syndrome) and is in a period of abstinence (Gowing et al., 1991; Rang et al., 2007).

A *blocking* medication (that is, an antagonist, see Chapter 2) will stop the drug of dependence from having an effect, and so removes the euphoric and other positive reinforcing effects. A prime example here is the use of naltrexone in the treatment of heroin dependence. An *aversive* medication produces an unpleasant reaction when it is used in combination with the drug of dependence but is safe when used by itself. An example is disulfiram, which when combined with alcohol produces vomiting, flushing and an unpleasant reaction to alcohol. Aversive agents replace the positive effects of a drug with negative consequences (that is, punishment), so motivating the person not to use the drug.

The final category of treatment involves a range of *psychosocial treatment* options. These approaches include counselling, support groups, social and welfare support and skills training. There are many health, legal, employment and other psychological problems that can arise from drug dependence. These problems can in themselves motivate a person to use drugs to cope. Addressing these problems can take a long time, and so as a result, many forms of psychosocial treatment will also take a long time. In general, these approaches are designed to address the psychological reasons for using drugs, support positive life changes, minimize the likelihood of relapse and build skills to assist with the attempt to quit the drug and cope with other aspects of life (Gowing et al., 2001; Jarvis, Tebbutt and Mattick, 1995; White, 1991). Often these approaches are combined with a medical treatment to provide a comprehensive treatment programme.

We will discuss each of these treatment categories in a little more detail later in this chapter. For now, let's look at general processes involved in the treatment of drug dependence.

There are a vast range of facilities available to receive treatment for drug dependence, each differing in the approaches offered, the philosophical approach to drug dependence and the professional background of the staff. For many people looking for assistance with their drug dependence, the first point of contact is often a general practitioner (GP). The GP may offer some specific treatment or may refer the person on to a specialist or specialist treatment centre.

Some specialist treatment facilities will include staff from a variety of professional backgrounds including medical doctors, nurses, psychiatrists, psychologists, social workers and so forth. Other facilities will have little input from medical staff and may include counsellors, psychologists or even former drug users.

Treatment facilities will also vary according to their source of funds. Some services rely upon payment from the individual, some may be government funded, while others may rely on charity donations (Lowinson, Ruiz and Millman, 1992; Melmon et al., 1992; White, 1991). Some facilities will offer outpatient programmes, some inpatient programmes and some both. Inpatient facilities are most often used for drug detoxification or treatment of specific medical complications of drug use. Such services are much more expensive to operate than outpatient programmes and, as a result, often only limited spaces are available. Treatment services may aim at achieving complete abstinence or they may aim to moderate and control the drug use to minimize harms to the individual and the broader community.

People enter into drug treatment through a number of different routes. These can include referral from a GP, criminal court, police officer, social worker or employer. Some individuals may enter treatment on a voluntary basis. Regardless of the route of entry into treatment, the first step in the treatment process is an assessment of the pattern of drug use and the other harms associated with dependence.

The initial assessment when entering treatment usually consists of an interview that is designed to understand the nature of the drug problem(s) and the associated harms. Topics covered may include the following: the reasons for entering treatment, the pattern and contexts of drug use, the degree of drug dependence, lifestyle and social stability, vocational and financial situation, family background and support, the involvement (if any) of significant others in treatment, mental health state and the stage of change. Often there will be a medical examination and a thorough assessment of any psychological problems (such as depression or anxiety) (for example Jarvis et al., 1995). A good treatment programme will identify all the areas where help is needed for each individual, and design a treatment programme that addresses each of these needs. An assessment of these factors will occur at the beginning of treatment and again at regular intervals during the course of treatment to monitor treatment effectiveness.

Let's turn our attention now to some of the specific treatment options available for drug dependence. We will begin with looking at the medical and pharmacological approaches to treatment and then move on to some of the most important psychosocial approaches. This overview is designed not to be a comprehensive exploration of these different approaches, but more to provide a summary of the different approaches that have been shown to be most effective in helping people deal with their addictive behaviour.

◉ The pharmacological and medical approach to treatment

The pharmacological approach to treatment entails the use of medication and other health support to manage the consequences, signs and symptoms, and medical complications of drug dependence. There are three key therapeutic issues arising from drug use and dependence, namely the consequences of *acute intoxication*, the management of the *physical withdrawal syndrome* and the management of *drug dependence*.

As we discussed in Chapter 2, most of the drugs of abuse and dependence will produce marked disturbances in the central nervous system. In many cases, intoxication on these drugs is also associated with disturbances in cardiovascular function. In order to manage the medical complications that can sometimes arising during intoxication, it is important to understand the pharmacology of the drug (Melmon et al., 1992; White, 1991). For example, opioid intoxication (or overdose as it is sometimes referred) will reduce the respiration rate to the extent that people can stop breathing. For stimulants such as amphetamines and cocaine, intoxication is associated with seizures, irregular heartbeat and sometimes psychosis and aggression. For drugs such as opioids and benzodiazepines, antidotes, in the form of antagonists (see Chapter 2), exist which can immediately reverse the drug effects. For other drugs no such antidotes exist, and so supportive medical treatment (such as anticonvulsants, cooling the body, sedatives and so on) is used.

As tolerance and physical dependence to a drug develops over time, a withdrawal syndrome may occur when there are low blood levels of the drug or it is abruptly stopped. These signs and symptoms of withdrawal can be very uncomfortable and sometimes (such as with alcohol), they can be life-threatening. These withdrawal signs and symptoms are generally the opposite of the drug effects that were initially sought by the drug user. For drugs such as alcohol, highly addicted drinkers can experience seizures during withdrawal that are life-threatening and require medical attention. Withdrawal symptoms can be stopped quickly by administering the drug, and for this reason motivate the person to seek and use the drug again (for example Rang et al., 2007).

Withdrawal represents the unopposed consequence of the adaptation in the central nervous system to the presence of the drug. As we discussed in Chapter 2, there are some key characteristics of tolerance and the withdrawal syndrome: firstly, if tolerance is developed to one drug, then tolerance will also be extended to all other drugs in that class. For example, developing a tolerance to heroin will mean that there is also tolerance to morphine, codeine, opium and so forth. Secondly, the concentration of the drug in the brain and the duration of its presence will affect the extent and rate of tolerance and neuroadaptation. The higher the usual dose of the drug and the shorter the half-life of the drug (its duration of action, see Chapter 2), the more intense the withdrawal syndrome. However, a drug with a longer half-life will lead to a less severe withdrawal syndrome but it will be experienced for a much longer time (Rang et al., 2007). For example, heroin, which has half-life of 3–6 hours, produces an intense withdrawal syndrome that will resolve within a few days. However, a longer acting opioid such as methadone (see below), which has a half-life of 24–36 hours, will produce a less severe withdrawal syndrome but it will persist for a few weeks.

The principles of cross-tolerance, and the role of the half-life on the intensity and duration of the withdrawal syndrome, provide a therapeutic strategy for managing the withdrawal syndrome. The primary pharmacological approach to the management of withdrawal syndromes includes treatment with an agonist drug that has a long half-life (for example Gowing et al., 2001). Some common examples are the use of methadone for heroin use and diazepam for alcohol. Patients are stabilized on the appropriate dose of the longer acting drug so that they don't experience withdrawal but also don't experience intoxication or euphoria. The dose of this drug is then slowly reduced until it is stopped altogether. If the reduction of dose is done slowly, the brain will have time to 'de-adapt' and so withdrawal symptoms are minimized. Other aspects of supportive care such as counselling and medical treatment for other health issues are also offered. In some cases, there may not be a suitable longer acting drug available; in which case, the signs and symptoms are medicated individually (for example, a pain reliever may be used for the aches and pains, while other medications are used to treat diarrhoea and so on).

As we discussed earlier in this chapter, the pharmacological management of drug dependence involves the longer-term use of a substitute but safer drug, or it involves the detoxification of the patient and the use of a blocking drug or an aversive drug. *Drug substitution treatment* involves the prescription of a drug with similar action to the drug of dependence but with a lower degree of risk (for example nicotine patches for those quitting smoking). The value of substitution treatment is that it removes the need for the individual to seek and use the harmful or illicit drug. By providing the drug in a safer form, the individual then has the opportunity to focus on other areas of their life, such as relationship problems, seeking employment or housing, resolving criminal issues and so forth (for example Gowing et al., 2001). Most importantly, by removing the need to buy illegal drugs, the individual has an opportunity to separate from their drug-using peers.

The rationale for using blocking and aversive agents with people who have stopped using the drug is to extinguish positive reinforcement from drug use. A *blocking agent* will prevent the drug of dependence from having an effect, and therefore will block the euphoric and other positive effects. An example is naltrexone for opioid dependence. An *aversive agent* produces an unpleasant reaction when used in combination with drugs of dependence but is safe when it is used by itself.

To demonstrate the pharmacological approach to treatment, let's look briefly at some examples for the major drugs of abuse.

Nicotine

Stopping smoking can be a very difficult process for many people. The best, and most successful, example of pharmacological treatment to assist with this is the use of nicotine replacement products such as gums and patches. Nicotine patches provide a slow release of nicotine to combat the cravings that occur during the withdrawal period. Nicotine gum does the same and can provide enough nicotine to combat the withdrawal symptoms. As the absorption of nicotine from gum and patches is quite slow, peak concentrations in the brain will be lower, and the rate of rise in blood levels of nicotine will be much slower than when cigarettes are smoked. Accordingly, an acute urge to smoke a cigarette, such as in stressful situations or in situations when the person would normally smoke (such as after a meal), may mean that these products aren't sufficient. Therefore, it is important that the person is also taught the skills to avoid these urges or situations (see below) (Gowing et al., 2001; White, 1991).

Alcohol

For a person who is severely dependent upon alcohol, the withdrawal syndrome can be life-threatening. The seizures, tremors and increased irregular heart rate are very serious conditions requiring medical assistance. For those requiring hospitalization, treatment will include supportive care and specific pharmacotherapy. Supportive care includes hydration, balancing of electrolyte abnormalities and dealing with the consequences of inadequate nutrition. Pharmacotherapy is designed to replace alcohol with a sedative drug that can be tapered slowly in a controlled manner. Benzodiazepines are the drug of choice as they alleviate the withdrawal symptoms and also minimize the likelihood of a seizure. Typically a long-acting benzodiazepine is provided (for example diazepam/valium), and then the dose is gradually reduced over the course of a few weeks (for example Gowing et al., 2001; White, 1991).

The primary example of the pharmacological treatment of dependence and the prevention of relapse is the use of the drug disulfiram (Antabuse). This drug inhibits the metabolism of alcohol in such a way as to produce a very unpleasant reaction if the person drinks alcohol (Rang et al., 2007). This reaction will include flushing of face, headache, nausea and vomiting. As a result, the person will not receive any positive reinforcement from drinking alcohol. However, to begin disulfiram (Antabuse) the person must first stop drinking and successfully detoxify (that is, successfully complete the withdrawal period) and this can be difficult. Also, it requires the person to continue taking the drug and not stop taking it if they feel the urge to consume alcohol. As a result, this treatment is most effective among those who are highly motivated to stop drinking or have a significant other person (such as a partner) to ensure that the medication is taken daily. Treatment with Antabuse will usually continue for at least a year (Gowing et al., 2001).

Opioids

The primary pharmacological approaches to treating heroin dependence involve either the substitution of heroin with a longer acting opioid, or detoxification followed by the use of a blocking agent (that is, an opioid antagonist).

While the heroin withdrawal syndrome is not life-threatening, it can be very unpleasant and detoxification can be difficult to achieve. The aim of the pharmacological treatment during this period is to ensure that the individual will complete withdrawal comfortably and safely. Treatment consists either of prescribing a longer acting opioid such as methadone and then slowly reducing the dose, or providing medications to treat each symptom individually. Evidence suggests that this treatment is associated with reasonable rates of completion of withdrawal, reduction of symptoms to tolerable levels and minimal adverse effects. However, there are high rates of relapse within the first two weeks of completing detoxification, indicating the need for follow-up treatment. Factors such as a stable home environment, support from family and friends and frequent contact with medical and support staff can improve completion rates (Gowing et al., 2001).

To manage heroin dependence over a longer term, pharmacological approaches will involve either opioid substitution treatment or the use of a blocking agent. The primary effective substitution therapy is called *methadone maintenance*. Methadone is an opioid that can be administered once a day to prevent the occurrence of a withdrawal syndrome. It is provided as a syrup that is swallowed, and, as such, blood concentrations will rise and fall slowly (see *routes of administration*, Chapter 2). The dosage of methadone is set so that it doesn't produce euphoria, but it will still alleviate withdrawal symptoms for 24 hours.

Methadone maintenance is a useful treatment option as it provides a controlled oral dose of a legal opioid. It has a much longer duration of action than heroin and therefore it can provide the person with an opportunity to separate from the drug subculture and lifestyle and achieve legal, social and financial security. Methadone programmes are very effective at reducing the physical and psychosocial harms associated with illicit drug use (Gowing et al., 2001). The benefits of methadone increase the longer the person remains in treatment and, for many people, they may need to receive methadone for a number of years.

An alternative approach is to use a blocking agent. Naltrexone is a long-acting opioid antagonist. It binds to the opioid receptor sites, displaces opioids from those sites and blocks opioid effects. As a result, a person will not experience any of the sought after positive effects of heroin. To commence on naltrexone, it is very important that the person has completely stopped using heroin, otherwise the withdrawal syndrome may occur. Naltrexone is very useful for people who are highly motivated to quit but less so for those who are less motivated (Gowing et al., 2001; White, 1991).

Cocaine and other psychostimulants

The continued use of cocaine and other stimulant drugs is motivated both by a craving for the high (positive reinforcement) and to relieve the depression and anxiety associated with chronic stimulant use (negative reinforcement) (Dyer and Cruickshank, 2005). The withdrawal syndrome from psychostimulants often involves depression and sadness, fatigue, hypersomnia followed by insomnia, drug craving and vivid, unpleasant dreams. In general, there is a lack of pharmacological treatment options for psychostimulants. To date, the most effective approach has been to medicate the troublesome symptoms and provide supportive care. Recently, researchers have examined the use of antidepressants to assist withdrawal with mixed results (Cruickshank et al., 2008). Hopefully, effective treatment options will be discovered in the near future.

Summary

In this book we have shown how addictive behaviour is a complex process, involving the interplay of pharmacology, learned factors and social setting. An understanding of the complex interrelationships of these factors is essential to successful treatment. Pharmacological treatments have been proved to be very successful in treating drug dependence, and this is especially true of the replacement treatments (that is, nicotine replacement therapy and heroin substitution treatment). However, it is rarely sufficient to provide only pharmacological treatment, and including a form of psychosocial therapy is often essential to address the psychosocial reasons for abusing a drug and the factors maintaining that drug abuse.

◉ Psychosocial interventions

Psychosocial therapies focus on the psychological, behavioural and social aspects of drug use. They may be offered as a standalone treatment or they may be offered with a pharmacological treatment. We will now briefly look at some of the available psychosocial interventions for drug dependence.

Counselling

Many people, particularly those who need assistance to get some order back into their lives, can benefit from counselling and support on an individual basis. A counsellor will build a trusting relationship without judgement, help the person develop a sense of responsibility and self-confidence, and assist the person to develop and implement their own solutions to their drug problems.

Counselling may be offered on an individual or group basis. Group counselling sessions give the opportunity to feel supported by other people experiencing similar problems and to practise skills in effective listening and communicating with others. As social factors play a significant role in the initiation and maintenance of drug use, counselling sessions may also help find solutions to problems in living conditions, relationships, job training and so forth. Counselling is rarely sufficient by itself to treat drug dependence but it is a vital addition to other forms of treatment (Gowing et al., 2001; Jarvis et al., 1995).

Motivational interviewing

Motivational interviewing is a specialized form of counselling. It involves an individual programme designed to help people move through the stages of change (see Chapter 1). It helps the person to make a decision to change their drug use while at the same time accepting the responsibility of that decision. At its most basic, it involves exploring the good things and less good things about drug use, and building upon any concerns of drug use. Motivational interviewing will create a 'psychological squirm' (see Saunders, Wilkinson and Allsop, 1991) where a person will face the discrepancy between themselves as an individual and themselves as a drug user. Often this provides a chance for the individual to become aware of those aspects of being a drug user that are not liked and this can become a powerful motivator for change.

Behaviourist approaches to treatment

There are a number of treatment options that are based upon the principles of behaviourism (see Chapter 3). The major principle is that drug use is a learned behaviour that can be 'un-learned' (White, 1991). Within this view, drug use is prompted by a number of antecedent events, such as certain social situations or moods, and is maintained by a number of possible reinforcers – the direct effects of the drug (an example of positive reinforcement), or the removal of discomfort such as in withdrawal (an example of negative reinforcement). Which of these reinforcers are important will depend upon the individual and the specific drug and may vary each time a drug is used.

One behaviourist approach is to examine the antecedent events for drug use and teach the individual to avoid them or handle them without taking drugs (see below). Alternatively, a medication may be used to alter the reinforcing properties of the drug (for example Antabuse for the use of alcohol).

An approach that has been shown to be effective within pharmacological treatments is called *contingency management*. This approach provides positive reinforcement contingent upon the person not taking the drug (Gowing et al., 2001). Abstinence, as checked by drug testing in urine, is rewarded with vouchers that can be exchanged for goods. This approach has been successfully used to keep people within comprehensive treatment programmes for heroin and cocaine dependence.

Cognitive behavioural approaches

Cognitive behavioural therapy is designed to help the person recognize the triggers for craving or using a drug and to modify any dysfunctional cognitions underlying drug-using behaviour (Jarvis et al., 1995). It typically involves skills training and practice to deal with craving, monitoring thoughts about drugs and monitoring high-risk situations associated with relapse.

Relaxation training

Relaxing training involves teaching the person a range of techniques to release stress and tension without resorting to drugs. People are taught how to relax in everyday situations where stress arises, and, recognizing tension when it exists, learning to relax the body. Techniques can include deep breathing, meditation, progressive muscle relaxation and so forth (Jarvis et al., 1995).

Drug refusal skills

Everybody faces situations where they experience social pressure to drink or use drugs. Teaching skills to refuse such offers with confidence can be an invaluable tool in preventing relapse. This form of skills training often involves discussions of body language, tone of voice, and specific examples of how to refuse a drug (Lowinson et al., 1992).

Assertiveness skills

This form of training is closely related to drug refusal skills training and helps an individual clearly express their own needs and emotions to others. For some people, the inability to communicate openly and directly leads to feelings of frustration, anger or distress and these feelings may contribute to the desire to use drugs. Role play is an essential part of teaching these skills, and so group settings are ideal. Topics covered in these programmes may include recognizing when one is not being assertive, and developing a variety of ways to deal appropriately with situations where the person has often found it difficult to express feelings, needs, wants and opinions directly and honestly without hostility or rudeness (Jarvis et al., 1995).

Problem solving skills

Problem solving skills training is designed to help the individual to deal with problems in everyday life without needing to use drugs. This may include recognizing when a problem exists, developing a variety of potential solutions, selecting the most appropriate, developing a plan to enact it and evaluating the effectiveness of the selected approach. It teaches people not to ignore problems or to let the pressure build up to the extent where drug use is seen as an easy and effective way to deal with that stress.

Cognitive restructuring

Cognitive restructuring involves teaching an individual to identify and challenge the thoughts and feelings that may lead to drug use. It is often effective when used with techniques that teach a behavioural skill, such as assertiveness training or drug refusal skills (Jarvis et al., 1991). These programmes will help people to recognize when they are thinking in a way that could lead to drug use, interrupt that train of thought, challenge the negative thoughts and then replace them with positive thoughts that do not involve drug use.

Many of the thoughts that lead to drug use can happen very quickly and the drug user may be unaware that they are occurring – that is, they are automatic thoughts (see Chapter 5). Often these thoughts are a result of how a person interprets events or the 'self talk' that occurs with an event. For example, a person who drops and breaks a dinner plate may immediately think 'I am stupid'. If unchecked, these thoughts can lead to feelings of anger, frustration or depression, which in turn may lead to drug use. The key step of cognitive restructuring is to help the person become aware of such negative thinking and reframe it into something more positive that will therefore be less likely to lead to the desire to take a drug (or engage in another addictive behaviour).

Relapse prevention training

Although many of the treatments described above have very high rates of success in stopping drug use in the short term, longer-term outcomes tend to be less impressive. After leaving a treatment programme, many people will find it difficult to resist the urge to take the drug. Relapse prevention training is a very useful approach that helps people learn how to avoid relapses and cope with relapses if they occur. It is considered an integral part of any treatment programme and has the general aim of ensuring people have a variety of skills and the confidence to avoid lapses to drug and alcohol use.

Most of this work was developed by Marlatt and Gordon (1985). According to their model, most relapses occur in a number of high-risk situations, namely interpersonal conflicts, social pressure to use a drug and negative emotional states. One of the major determinants of whether an individual copes with a high-risk situation is their expectancy of success – people who have more optimism and confidence are more likely to be successful in resisting the urge to use a drug. This expectancy is shaped by prior experience, and so any relapse may reduce self-efficacy and increase feelings of guilt and pessimism.

Relapse prevention training attempts to challenge common beliefs about giving up addictive behaviours. It is designed to reduce the impact of a failure by emphasizing the behaviour change is not an all or nothing event – rather it is a process whereby learning from mistakes forms part of the process to achieving a drug-free state. Lifestyle factors that can either hinder or support behaviour change are examined, and the reasons and benefits for stopping drug use are explored. High-risk situations are identified and described in terms of where, when, with whom, doing what and feeling what. Once identified, particular skills may be taught to effectively respond to these high-risk situations.

As such, this therapeutic approach is designed to minimize the chances of a relapse and to control it once it has begun. For each high-risk situation, a person is taught to either avoid the situation or learn to cope with it. The therapist's job is to help identify these situations and then provide the skills to cope with them in a drug-free manner. Relapse prevention should be an integral part of all treatment options for addictive behaviours (Gowing et al., 2001; White, 1991).

Peer support programmes

Peer support programmes (also known as self help groups) offer ongoing social support to people who are attempting to stop drug use. They are offered by people who have themselves previously experienced drug problems. They may include assistance from trained medical or psychological staff, or they may be self-operated. The two most common peer support programmes are therapeutic communities and Alcoholics Anonymous.

Therapeutic communities

Therapeutic communities are based on the principle that a structured drug-free residential setting provides the best context to address the underlying causes of drug dependence. These programmes assist the individual to develop appropriate skills and attitudes to make positive changes. Most programmes require the individual to live in the community for a period of time, often in the range of three to six months. While this time commitment can be difficult for some people, for others it provides a needed break from the environments and situations associated with the addictive behaviour.

Therapeutic communities are operated by people in the process of reducing drug use, former drug-dependent people who serve as counsellors and, in some cases, professionals who organize the community (Gowing et al., 2001). Therapeutic communities emphasize the acceptance of personal responsibility for decisions and actions and assign residents tasks of everyday living (such as gardening, cooking and so forth). By participating in a therapeutic community, drug users can leave their usual environments and so avoid many of the high-risk situations that prompt their use of drugs. For some people, this approach can be very helpful in dealing with drug dependence.

12 Step Programmes – Alcoholics Anonymous

Alcoholics Anonymous is the oldest and most well known of the self-help approaches, and variants exist for illicit drugs (Narcotics Anonymous) and for the families of alcohol dependent people (Alanon). These programmes are designed to help a person achieve abstinence from drug use one day at a time through the social support offered at meetings. The programmes are based upon the disease concept of drug dependence (see Chapter 1) and so hold the view that drug dependence is an illness that cannot be cured, only arrested.

Programmes such as these are referred to as *12-Step Programmes*. Broadly speaking the 12-steps involve the following principles: admitting powerlessness over a drug, connecting with a God or higher being, admitting one's moral failings, admitting the harms done to other people by the drug use and then making amends. Essentially, the key steps to maintaining abstinence are to admit one's own powerlessness over the drug and develop a strong spiritual belief system (Gowing et al., 2001; White, 1991). This carries the implication that a decision to change is within the power of the individual, even if the power to successfully achieve that change is not.

One of the perceived benefits of these programmes is that they provide an opportunity to develop alternative social networks that do not engage in the addictive behaviour. However, assessing the effectiveness of these programmes is very difficult and very few evaluations have been published (Gowing et al., 1991). This is partly because a central tenet of these programmes is anonymity and so the collection of personal information and research is discouraged. Nonetheless, it is apparent that some people can benefit from this approach. Regular attendance and participating in group meetings (not just attendance) are key factors for success.

⊙ Evaluating treatments: Do they work?

To overcome our impression that 'everything works', and to improve treatment outcomes generally and treatment allocation procedures specifically, we have to open the black box to understand the processes of change and the factors which stimulate or impede them. (Bühringer and Pfeiffer-Gerschel, 2008)

Thus far we have considered some of the wide range of treatments that are available for the treatment of addictive behaviours, including the pharmacological interventions such as methadone maintenance, which are aimed at replacing a drug of abuse or blocking its effect, to psychosocial interventions, which seek to support the individual and help them to build skills and understanding of their problematic patterns of behaviour.

The key question that needs to be asked of any intervention is whether it is effective: does it work? There have been a number of large-scale trials that have attempted to address this question, which we will discuss in more detail below, but first we must spend a moment considering what it actually means to say that an intervention has *worked*. While a seemingly obvious question – our first instinct would be to suggest that an intervention in this area has worked if the individual has stopped drinking/smoking/gambling/and so on – the problem of addictive behaviour is much more than just engagement in the behaviour per se. When weighing up the effectiveness and efficiency of an intervention, health service providers (in particular, *health economists*, see Thinking scientifically box below) have to consider the costs of treatment in relation to the savings that it produces (that is, its cost–effectiveness). Are the benefits to individuals and society justified by the outcomes? For instance, if an individual is significantly more likely to return to work as well as maintaining abstinence after a particular treatment, we would consider this treatment to be more effective than another that only leads to reductions in use, but leaves the individual (perhaps physically or emotionally) unable to reintegrate into a work environment. It is in this context that many of the major treatment approaches have been evaluated, and to which we will now turn our attention.

Thinking scientifically → **The economy of health: weighing up the costs and benefits of treatment**

Health economics is that branch of economics (sometimes referred to as *medical economics*) which is concerned with estimating the full economic costs of illnesses and treatments. Whether a treatment leads to a reduction in an addictive behaviour is one thing, whether it is cost-effective is quite another.

If money was no object, it is conceivable that we could literally cure a range of addictive behaviours, by developing interventions that perhaps involved assigning 24-hour guards to ensure that the individual did not relapse. Aside from the fact that in any health service money is indeed an object (and a finite one at that), the 'problem' with addictive behaviours is not in fact singular and linked only to the individual using or engaging in the behaviour. Quite to the contrary, many addictive behaviours involve breaking the law (for example seeking out and buying controlled substances; engaging in acquisitive crimes to fund a habit and so on), may often lead to the individual being unable to find or keep a job, and can of course lead to serious long-term health conditions (for example liver cirrhosis among dependent drinkers, blood borne infections such as hepatitis C and HIV among injecting drug users). These things, among many other similar factors, have an economic impact upon society – and together with the price tag of any intervention, make up the full costs of addictive behaviours.

To understand just how great such associated costs can be, Gossop, Marsden and Stewart (2001) have shown that in a sample of 1075 drug users, the estimated costs of their criminal activities during a single year were around £5m. Therefore, an intervention can be thought of as effective to the extent that it, in addition to reducing engagement in the behaviour, also improves employment prospects, reduces the likelihood of long-term ill health, and so forth. Simply saying that an intervention 'works' because it leads to reductions in drug use is not an appropriate way of measuring success – neither for society as a whole nor for the individuals who are accessing the treatment. As we stated at the beginning of this chapter, it has been estimated that for every £1.00 spent on providing treatment, there is a £2.50 saving to the community in terms of reduced costs of policing, and health and social welfare services (Davies et al., 2009) – and for this reason we can be confident in saying that 'treatment works'.

In 1989, the largest ever clinical trial of psychotherapies, funded by the US National Institute on Alcohol Abuse and Alcoholism began. Project MATCH (Matching Alcoholics to Treatment based on Client Heterogeneity) set out to assess whether careful matching of 1726 alcohol-dependent patients to one of three different forms of treatment (12-step facilitation, cognitive behavioural therapy, or motivational enhancement therapy) would lead to improved treatment outcomes at a one-year follow-up, compared to patients who were randomly assigned to one of the three treatments (Project MATCH Research Group, 1997).

The surprising finding from Project MATCH was that treatment matching had no significant effect on treatment outcomes, and that all three treatment types produced near-identical recovery rates. In a follow-up analysis of Project MATCH outcomes, Cutler and Fishbain (2005) went further to suggest that treatments only accounted for around 3 per cent of drinking outcomes, and that many of the participants who dropped out of the trial demonstrated significant improvements having received no treatment at all. A more recent clinical trial, the UK Alcohol Treatment Trial (UKATT), found similar evidence when assigning patients to both a standard and newly developed psychosocial intervention (UKATT Research Team, 2005). While treatment was associated with generally positive drinking outcomes, there were no discernible differences in outcome between the treatments themselves.

While MATCH and UKATT were designed as formal clinical trials, aimed at evaluating specific and circumscribed psychosocial treatments, two further studies, the National Treatment Outcome Research Study (NTORS; see for example Gossop, Marsden, Stewart and Kidd, 2003) and the Drug Treatment Outcome Research Study (DTORS; see for example Davies et al., 2009) were designed to assess the effectiveness of treatment as a whole by following drug misusers as they passed through existing treatment services in the UK. Like MATCH and UKATT, both NTORS and DTORS demonstrated that treatments for drug dependence were effective – in NTORS, more than 25 per cent of opiate users who underwent community-based treatment, and 38 per cent who underwent residential treatment, were totally abstinent from all drugs at a five-year follow-up. DTORS reported similarly positive findings, that drug treatment has additional beneficial effects, beyond simply reducing drug use, in the sense of reducing drug use and criminal behaviour, and improving social and personal functioning.

So the evidence seems to be quite convincing – both psychosocial and pharmacotherapeutic interventions 'work' in the sense that many people who engage with them experience significant reductions in drug or alcohol use and improved quality of life, and essentially become more independent individuals. On the evidence that both psychosocial and pharmacological interventions have been shown to be effective, it is not a great leap of faith to assume that a combination of the two, where appropriate, might be doubly effective. Project COMBINE (Combined Pharmacotherapies and Behavioural Interventions for Alcohol Dependence, COMBINE Study Research Group, 2003) was set up specifically to test this idea. In this clinical trial, 1383 harmful drinkers who met the criteria for alcohol dependence were assigned to receive a pharmacotherapeutic intervention (naltrexone and/or acamprosate), a behavioural intervention (comprising elements of cognitive behavioural therapy, 12-step and motivational interviewing), or a combination of the two. While during active treatment the combination of naltrexone (but not acamprosate) and the behavioural intervention seemed to have positive effects on drinking behaviour, these effects had all but disappeared at a one-year follow-up. Moreover, there was also some evidence that participants receiving both the behavioural intervention and a placebo medication showed greater improvements over those receiving only the behavioural intervention.

It is within the context of this collection of findings, particularly from COMBINE, that Bühringer and Pfeiffer-Gerschel (2008) made the comment which opened this section. Fundamentally, there is no escaping the evidence that treatments for addictive behaviours work – even in the broader and more stringent sense of 'working' required to make an intervention cost-effective. The problems can be summarized as follows:

- None of the commonly available treatments seem to be any better than others
- It is not clear on what basis one form of treatment should be prescribed to an individual over another form, or indeed if this matters at all
- When people show improvements, we cannot explain why
- When people fail to improve, we cannot say why

To paraphrase Bühringer and Pfeiffer-Gerschel, we need to look into the black box of recovery to understand what it is about our treatments that makes them work in order to make them work better.

Summary

A thorough description of all the different types of pharmacological and psychosocial therapies is beyond the scope of this book. In general, each of these programmes will be effective for different individuals. Furthermore, multicomponent or comprehensive treatment programmes that address both the behavioural and the biological (that is, pharmacological) aspects of drug dependence will be generally more effective than a single treatment approach alone. It may take a number of attempts at treatment before success is finally achieved, but participating in any treatment programme can reduce the harms associated with addictive behaviours and reduce the associated costs to society.

◉ Further reading

Begg, E. (2001) *Clinical Pharmacology Essentials* (2nd edn). Auckland: ADIS International.

Cruickshank, C. and Dyer, K.R. (2009) A review of the clinical pharmacology of methamphetamine. *Addiction*, 104, 1085–99.

Gowing, L., Proudfoot, H., Henry-Edwards, S. and Teeson, M. (2001) *Evidence Supporting Treatment. The Effectiveness of Interventions for Illicit Drug Use*. ACT: Australian National Council on Drugs.

Jarvis, T., Tebbutt, J. and Mattick, R. (1995) *Treatment Approaches for Alcohol and Drug Dependence. An Introductory Guide*. Brisbane: John Wiley & Sons.

White, J.M. (1991) *Drug Dependence*. Englewood Cliffs, NJ: Prentice Hall.

Chapter 7

Primary prevention options for addictive behaviours

Introduction

In the previous chapter we provided a brief overview of some of the different treatment options that are available for people attempting to stop their addictive behaviour. However, treatment is designed to aid individuals who have already developed a problem. As the adage goes, **prevention** is better than cure, and this will be the focus of the present chapter.

In this chapter we will examine:
- Different strategies for preventing the development of addictive behaviours
- The different elements of prevention programmes
- The role of the media in the delivery of prevention programmes

Treatment is often a frustrating experience for the clinician because of the high relapse rate among many of the participants. For those with dependencies, often a number of treatment attempts, possibly involving different types of treatment, are required before complete success is achieved. The cost of delivering comprehensive treatment programmes can be very expensive, although they do lead to significant savings in other realms of policing and social welfare (that is, treatment is cost-effective). Nonetheless, in an ideal situation, we would prevent people from developing addictive behaviours and prevent drug experimentation and usage becoming problematic.

If we believe that addictive behaviour is not something one is 'born with' (see Thinking scientifically – Genetics and addictive behaviours, Chapter 2) and therefore can't avoid, then we can start to consider ways to prevent addictive behaviour from developing to the point where treatment is required. However, it is very difficult to develop and evaluate effective prevention strategies, and it can be quite a challenge to counteract the positive images of drug use and other addictive behaviours (for example gambling) that are so pervasive in the media. This chapter will describe some of the strategies that have been developed to prevent people from developing addictive behaviours.

Primary prevention strategies

We can broadly describe prevention strategies within three categories. **Primary prevention** strategies are designed to reach individuals before they have developed an addictive behaviour. They target individuals who have not yet begun using alcohol and other drugs, or started gambling and so forth. Their goal is to challenge the individual and/or environmental factors that promote unhealthy behaviour. This chapter will focus upon an overview of primary prevention strategies.

Secondary prevention strategies involve screening and detecting drug use and other addictive behaviours at an early stage in order to intervene before significant problems have developed. Examples of secondary prevention strategies include roadside alcohol and drug testing of drivers and pre-employment, random or probable cause (that is, after an accident or other incident) drug testing in the workplace (Dyer and Wilkinson, 2008).

Tertiary prevention strategies are designed to prevent addictive behaviour developing further and minimize the likelihood of serious medical and psychosocial consequences associated with drug dependence. The prevalence of alcohol and other drug use in society and the risks associated with this use, such as hepatitis and HIV/AIDS as well as psychosocial harms, mean that tertiary prevention strategies are important.

Prevention strategies take place on many different levels and cover many different forms. They can be broadly conceptualized in terms of having the goals of supply reduction or demand reduction. *Supply reduction* efforts are based on the assumption that drug use and other addictive behaviours can be managed by controlling how easily they can be obtained. This is the major approach of drug law enforcement agencies. *Demand reduction* efforts are those that attempt to discourage individuals from using and abusing drugs or engaging in other unhealthy behaviours. Demand reduction includes prevention, education and treatment strategies.

Prevention strategies can be designed to reach an individual or an entire society. However, the history of prevention programmes has not been impressive. There are few programmes that have been shown to have had a significant effect and indeed, very few evaluations have been conducted. However, recently there has been some cause for optimism, and strategies that combine effective education with legal limitations have been shown to reduce the harms associated with much addictive behaviour.

Types of primary prevention

Primary prevention efforts can be broadly divided into six general strategies. The first are *information dissemination approaches* which aim to educate people of the harms associated with addictive behaviours. These approaches may include messages designed to promote fear (for example fear of death if one drinks and then drives a motor vehicle) or promote moral behaviour. The second type of strategy involves *personal growth* and includes programmes that are designed to promote self-esteem and develop social skills. *Alternative approaches* involve providing activities in the community to reduce boredom and provide an alternative to the addictive behaviour. The fourth strategy involves programmes that are designed to develop *skills for resisting* addictive behaviours, such as drug refusal skills. The next set of strategies focus upon *personal and social skills training* and include programmes that are designed to improve self-esteem without necessarily focusing upon an addictive behaviour. The final strategy involves *public health approaches,* which are directed at the general population rather than a specific age group. This approach includes legislative controls on the availability and price of drugs (for example) coupled with educational campaigns delivered through the mass media.

Prevention strategy	Goals	Examples of methods
Information dissemination	Increase knowledge about the consequences of drug abuse, promoting anti-drug attitudes	Presentations in the classroom or community, displays and posters, pamphlets, adverts in mass media and so on
Personal growth	Increase self-esteem, responsible decision making, personal growth; often includes little or no information about drugs	Outdoor or community activities, group problem solving activities
Alternative activities	Increase self-esteem, self-reliance, provide viable alternatives reduce boredom and sense of alienation	Youth centres, recreational activities, vocational training and so on
Resistance skills	Increase awareness of social influences and develop skills for resisting these influences	Discussion, skills training, promoting positive peer influences
Personal and social skills training	Increase decision making, anxiety reduction, assertiveness training	Discussion and skills training
Public health approaches	To reduce the harms associated with addictive behaviours in the community	Legislation to restrict access to alcohol and drugs, drink-driving laws, taxation policies

Table 7.1 General strategies of primary prevention

Information dissemination

A common form of prevention is to provide education to young people to promote awareness of the risks associated with alcohol and other drugs before dependence has developed. These programmes provide factual information about drugs and their adverse effects, but often emphasize the adverse effects to promote fear. They are designed to change attitudes and provide a basis on which young people can make rational decisions. That is, they are based on the view that addictive behaviour is the result of insufficient knowledge of the adverse consequences, but once provided with this knowledge, people will make rational and healthy decisions. It is also assumed that this information will develop attitudes that will lead to healthy behaviours.

Information dissemination prevention strategies often take the form of public information campaigns (such as adverts, posters and so on) and school-based programmes (including classroom curricula, guest speakers and educational films). Many use a fear-arousal approach rather than a simple statement of facts. However, evidence suggests that these approaches are generally not effective and may sometimes lead to an increase in the behaviour that they were designed to prevent.

Personal growth

These programmes are designed to develop personal skills and maturity. They place less emphasis on factual information about the adverse consequences and focus more upon personal and social development. They promote self-understanding and acceptance through activities such as values clarification and responsible decision making, improving interpersonal relations by building effective communication, peer counselling and assertiveness. Unfortunately their effectiveness has also been disappointing; while these programmes have often been able to impact upon some of the attitudes toward drug use and other addictive behaviours, they haven't reliably demonstrated an impact on the actual behaviours themselves.

Providing an alternative activity

These strategies are designed to provide young people with alternatives to drug use and other addictive behaviours. For example, this might involve the opening of youth centres that provide a variety of activities (sports, hobbies, academic tutoring and so on). The assumption is that if provided with appealing alternative activities, it is less likely that young people will engage in drug use or other unhealthy behaviours. Similarly, programmes might target how a young person may feel about themselves and others, and offer a range of activities that promote teamwork, self-confidence and self-esteem. Again, while these programmes may benefit some individuals, they do not seem to be broadly effective in reducing addictive behaviour.

Resistance skills training

These programmes are designed to increase awareness of the various social pressures to engage in drug use and other unhealthy behaviours. They place emphasis on teaching specific skills to effectively resist both peer and media pressure to use a drug. The psychosocial prevention strategies that use this technique are based on a model that highlights the fundamental importance of social factors in promoting the initiation of drug abuse and other unhealthy behaviours among young people (that is, peer pressure and modelling of behaviour from others; attitudes contained in the media).

Resistance skills training approaches generally teach individuals how to recognize situations where there is a risk of peer pressure to use a drug or engage in other unhealthy behaviours. Participants are either taught to identify and then avoid high risk situations, or they are taught skills to effectively cope with these situations. Other common components of these types of strategies include the use of peer leaders (for example older students) or they provide factual information to challenge the belief that drug use is widespread (for example by presenting national prevalence data). These programmes have been shown to have some effect on limiting drug use.

Personal and social skills training

Personal and social skills training approaches to prevention are based upon social learning theory and problem behaviour theory (see Chapter 3). Drug abuse and other addictive behaviours are conceptualized as socially learned and functional, resulting from the interplay of social, environmental and personal factors. That is, addictive behaviour is a 'learned' behaviour, developed through modelling and reinforcement and influenced by cognitions, attitudes and beliefs.

Typically these programmes will include at least one of the following strategies:

- General problem solving and decision-making skills
- Cognitive skills for resisting interpersonal or media influences
- Skills to increase self-esteem and assertiveness
- Skills to reduce stress and anxiety through the use of cognitive coping skills or behavioural relaxation techniques
- General social skills

These programmes are designed to teach young people the skills for coping with life that will have a broad application and do not necessarily focus on drug abuse or a specific addictive behaviour. Such approaches have been shown to have significant effects on reducing the harms associated with alcohol and drug use.

Thinking scientifically → **A comment on education approaches in the prevention of addictive behaviours**

The weight of evidence appears to suggest that drug education approaches, especially those that promote the adverse effects of drugs and other addictive behaviours, are generally not effective, whereas those that teach more general social skills show some promise.

This finding was first demonstrated, in the Netherlands, by De Haes and Schuurman in 1975 (De Haes and Schuurman, 1975; 1987). They compared the effectiveness of three different approaches to drug education designed to prevent the use of cannabis. One approach focused on fear arousal and the moral dimensions of cannabis use; one focused on providing information about the effects of cannabis and other drugs; the third approach did not specifically focus on drugs but rather gave pupils the opportunity to discuss the broader problems of adolescence. It was found that none of the approaches deterred those who had already used cannabis. Indeed, among those who received the drug-specific education there was an increase in drug experimentation that was more than twice that of a monitored group who did not receive any of the programmes. However, with the third, more general approach, there was a slightly higher reduction in the numbers experimenting with cannabis than one would normally have expected if nothing had been done.

In recent times there has been some cause for optimism. The recent EU-DAP study (European Drug Addiction Prevention Trial) (Faggiano and EU-DAP Study Group, 2010) involved 170 schools (7079 pupils, aged 12–14 years, in seven European countries). Students were randomly assigned to one of three different types of prevention programme or a control condition. It was found that the school curriculum that was based upon the social influence approach had some effects in delaying the onset of alcohol abuse and cannabis use, but not for cigarette smoking. These results are encouraging but show that no prevention strategy will ever be 100 per cent effective in eliminating the harms that arise from an addictive behaviour.

Public health approaches

The public health approach to preventing addictive behaviour includes campaigns that are directed at the general population rather than necessarily being solely focused on a specific age group. The focus is often on reducing the harms to the individual and broader community of addictive behaviours. This approach balances demand reduction and supply reduction goals, while including a commitment to harm reduction (that is, reducing the harms associated with addictive behaviours).

For example, this approach balances school and public health education with regulatory limitations such as advertising, drink-drive laws, hours of opening for hotels, drug classification and so forth. The focus though is not on the criminal aspects of drug use but the health aspects. Prevention strategies within this approach include making some drugs illegal, controlling the availability and price of legal drugs, placing high taxes on some drugs, and providing educational campaigns through the mass media.

The use of the mass media to provide primary prevention

The media can be a powerful means of influencing attitudes, beliefs, norms and behaviours associated with addictive behaviour. Even the most cursory analysis of films, television and radio will show the pervasiveness of drug content. Advertising in particular may often include images that create a positive attitude towards alcohol and other addictive behaviours. Often the messages that promote safer drug use (for example) are less obvious than those promoting the more appealing aspects. Over the years there have been a number of mass media campaigns developed to prevent the harms associated with drug use, and many have taken an information dissemination or fear arousal approach.

There has been relatively little research evaluating the effect of such public health messages and the results from the research that has been conducted have often been disappointing. While some campaigns have increased knowledge and affected attitudes, others, especially those that focus on promoting fear, have had no effect or may have actually increased drug use (Flay and Sobel, 1983).

Many advertisements for alcohol now include messages to promote safer drinking behaviour. The evidence suggests that it is very unlikely that these messages have a significant impact on drinking behaviour. For example, a recent experiment used equipment to monitor the eye movements of young people as they looked at print advertisements for alcohol (Thomsen and Fulton, 2007). The responsibility or moderation messages contained within these advertisements were the least frequently viewed textual or visual areas looked at by the students, equating to 0.35 seconds or approximately 7 per cent of the total viewing time. Among those who did look at the advertisements' safety message, less than a quarter could remember what it said.

There is good reason to believe that including fear arousal messages will not be effective in reducing the harms associated with addictive behaviours. *Terror management theory* (Greenberg, Solomon and Pyszczynski, 1997) demonstrates that a focus on mortality-related risks in prevention programmes may actually lead to an increase in that behaviour if it is important to a person's self-esteem. For example, information campaigns that highlight the risk of death after drinking and driving may actually increase the likelihood of drink-driving, if driving is important to that person's self-esteem (Jessop, Albery, Rutter and Garrod, 2008).

The evidence suggests that prevention campaigns that promote the adverse consequences of addictive behaviours must also present information that can assist the person in changing their behaviour, and this information must be presented in a non-threatening manner (for example Witte, 1992). To be effective, mass media campaigns must place greater emphasis on promoting strategies to combat the social and environmental influences that promote drug use and other addictive behaviours, rather than merely highlighting the possible adverse consequences.

The role of supply reduction legislation

To explore the role of legislation and legal controls within prevention strategies, it is useful to look at the example of policies designed to limit the harms associated with drinking alcohol. Implementing legislation that controls the price and taxation for legal drugs is aimed both at raising funds to finance the health programme and also at reducing consumption. Examples for alcohol include limiting the opening hours of pubs, taxing according to the alcohol content of various products, labelling alcoholic products with the alcohol content (in terms of units of alcohol) that they contain, controlling the places and hours of opening of venues to purchase alcohol, and strictly enforcing the illegal sale of alcohol to minors.

The focus on harm reduction through clear labelling of alcohol content on products and guidance concerning safe levels of alcohol carries with it the assumption that providing such information and facilitating its comprehension will reduce irresponsible drinking behaviour. Unfortunately this is not always the case. A recent study of the drinking behaviour of medical students at a London university showed that nearly 80 per cent of students consumed alcohol in a hazardous manner and approximately 40 per cent were at risk of developing alcohol dependence. This high-risk drinking behaviour was despite the fact that all of the students could correctly report current UK drinking guidelines (2–3 units of alcohol/day for women and 3–4 units of alcohol/day for men), and all had received a structured curriculum incorporating specific education on alcohol and other drug misuse (Moss, Dyer and Albery, 2009).

This study demonstrated that accurate comprehension of current sensible drinking guidelines was not associated with sensible drinking behaviour or willingness to moderate consumption within recommended limits. The fact that the students comprised individuals who would be expected to understand the health implications of unsafe drinking, and who will be delivering care to patients experiencing alcohol-related harm in the future, further undermines the assertion that knowledge of sensible drinking guidelines and enhanced understanding of the consequences of not adhering to these guidelines will lead to more sensible drinking behaviour. Indeed, there is evidence that such guidance may even be strategically misused by some. Following the introduction of mandatory standard drink labelling throughout Australia in 1995, after many years of concerted policy-driven research, researchers found that younger drinkers actually used this information so that they would know which drinks were the strongest, at the lowest price (Jones and Gregory, 2009).

Government policies that set limitations on the purchase and consumption of alcohol, and, where appropriate, enforce legislative measures, appear to be effective (Anderson, Chisholm and Fuhr, 2009) and cost-effective (Doran et al., 2008) in reducing alcohol-related harm. In general, taxing alcoholic products based on the amount of alcohol they contain, labelling these products with the alcohol content and safe drinking messages, and educating the public on safe drinking (that is, how much alcohol is damaging to health) are all important first steps in tackling alcohol-related harm. However, although they may reduce the overall prevalence of alcohol-related harm in the community, some people will still experience significant drinking problems despite these prevention strategies. As a result, there remains a need to conduct research to develop more effective prevention strategies and also improve the available treatment options.

◉ Chapter summary

Prevention programmes have had mixed success in reducing addictive behaviour in the community. While many school-based education programmes will not effectively reduce drug-related harm, public information and education programmes can increase attention to drug issues. Legislation and government policies that regulate the availability and accessibility of alcohol and other drugs can reduce population alcohol-related harm but will not entirely eliminate unsafe behaviour (Moss et al., 2009). The banning of alcohol and other drug-related advertising, drink-driving countermeasures and individually directed interventions directed at those already at risk are also effective in reducing the overall prevalence of alcohol and other drug-related harm (Anderson et al., 2009). However, there remains a need to develop and evaluate more effective prevention strategies. In the next chapter, we will discuss how advances in our understanding of the psychological and biological characteristics of addictive behaviour may provide clues to guide the development of more effective prevention and treatment programmes.

◉ Further reading

Anderson, P., Chisholm, D. and Fuhr, D. (2009) Effectiveness and cost-effectiveness of policies and programmes to reduce the harm caused by alcohol. *The Lancet*, 373, 2234–46.

Botvin, G.J. and Botvin, E.M. (1992) School-based and community-based prevention approaches. In Lowinson, J.H., Ruiz, P. and Millman, R.B. (eds) (1992) *Substance Abuse. A Comprehensive Textbook*. Baltimore: Williams & Wilkins.

De Haes, W. and Schuurman, J. (1987) Looking for effective drug education programmes: Exploration of the effects of different drug reduction programmes. *Health Education Research*, 2(4): 433–8.

Gill, J. and O'May, F. (2006) How 'sensible' is the UK Sensible Drinking message? Preliminary findings amongst newly matriculated female university students in Scotland. *Journal of Public Health*, 29, 13–16.

Jonas, S. (1992) Public health approach to the prevention of substance abuse. In Lowinson, J.H., Ruiz, P., Millman, R.B. (eds) *Substance Abuse. A Comprehensive Textbook*. Baltimore: Williams & Wilkins.

Chapter 8

Integrating addictive behaviour

👁 Introduction

Throughout this book we have described a broad range of theoretical perspectives that attempt to explain various aspects of the development, maintenance, treatment and prevention of addictive behaviour. Each model has its own strengths for some aspects of addictive behaviour, but to date there has been no single unified theory that adequately covers all the determinants and consequences of addictive behaviour. If one thing is certain from all the material we have covered, it is that addictive behaviours are complex, and our tools for both treating and preventing them need to reflect this. This inherent complexity reflects the fact that a complete understanding of addictive behaviour absolutely has to include an appreciation of the biological, psychological (cognitive and behavioural) and environmental factors that are involved.

> **In this chapter we will examine:**
> - The importance of biological, psychological and environmental factors in addictive behaviour
> - A new model for integrating these three types of influence in a coherent fashion
> - The practical utility of this new model for understanding addictive behaviour, predicting its consequences, and identifying suitable treatment and prevention intitiatives

In this chapter we will present a model that attempts to integrate the existing theoretical perspectives and research evidence, and identify some future directions for research, treatment and prevention. The framework that we will present is built around the dual systems framework for cognitive functioning, which was introduced in Chapter 5 but also incorporates many of the different theories that we have presented in this book.

To recap, dual systems theory posits two distinct information-processing systems in the human mind. System 1 is the automatic, and often unconscious, default processing mechanism, responsible for large amounts of our everyday thought and behaviour. System 2, on the other hand, deals with the more conscious, effortful and rule-based information processing, which is engaged most typically when we are faced with complex and novel problems. System 2 processing can be impaired by engaging in an addictive behaviour (for example drug intoxication or the thrill of gambling), whereas System 1 processing is relatively stable (Moss and Albery, 2009).

We have broken down the various factors (or inputs) involved in the development, maintenance and treatment of addictive behaviour into three distinct categories. The first category of factors that we know are involved in addictive behaviours is the *biological* domain. That is, the processes of drug action and drug effect, tolerance and withdrawal, leading to the development of physical dependence, which motivates continued use. Second, we have identified a category that will be labelled *psycho-behavioural*, which includes the emotional, reinforcing and learned factors that underpin psychological dependence. Finally, we will discuss *socio-environmental* factors, which include the legal status of the drug, the attitudes of other people, pricing and availability of drugs, and the environmental context in which the addictive behaviour is based. At the centre of the model we have placed the System 1 and System 2 cognitive processes, which process the information from each of the three categories of inputs and lead to a response of either engaging in the addictive behaviour or not. The responses made to an input (for example entering an environment where drugs are available, taking a drug, or experiencing a withdrawal syndrome) will also, in turn, become an input that generates another response (such as buying the drug and becoming intoxicated, consuming more of the drug than initially intended, or finding a dealer to buy more of the drugs).

We will now look at each of these categories in turn and describe their role within our framework for understanding the development and maintenance of addictive behaviour, and then consider how the three interlink to produce a coherent framework for understanding addictive behaviours. We will conclude this chapter, and the book, by discussing the treatment and prevention implications of this framework.

⟨◉⟩ Biological factors

The biological features of drug dependence are fundamental for gaining a full understanding of addictive behaviour and developing appropriate treatment and prevention approaches. Each of the drugs of abuse will release dopamine in the reward pathway, and so produce a positive effect that reinforces their continued use. It is highly likely that other addictive behaviours, such as gambling, are also reinforced in part through the process of dopamine-induced activation of the reward pathway. The chronic use of most drugs of dependence will lead to the development of tolerance, whereby the drug has a reduced effect over time, and withdrawal, whereby absence of the drug leads to physiological discomfort and motivates further use. The direct effects of a drug, the release of dopamine in the reward pathway and the discomfort of the withdrawal syndrome, represent some of the physiological inputs that we may process (cognitively) before engaging in a behaviour.

Figure 8.1 illustrates the beginning of our framework. Some biological inputs can directly lead to a response. Other biological inputs can be processed by the cognitive processing system and can then lead to a response or change in the intensity of the response. Let's look at the example of the physical withdrawal syndrome. Firstly, absence of a drug (that is, no drug at the site of action) will, in a physically dependent person, produce a withdrawal syndrome. In this example, the absence of the drug is the biological input and the withdrawal syndrome is the response. The nature of that withdrawal syndrome – what symptoms are experienced and the timing of those symptoms – is governed by the drug itself. Each of the drugs of abuse has a defined withdrawal syndrome that is always the opposite of the drug effects (see Chapter 2) and there is no need for any cognitive involvement for the withdrawal syndrome to be experienced.

However, Figure 8.1 also shows that biological inputs can enter the cognitive processing system. In this example, the *intensity* of the withdrawal syndrome can be affected by cognitive processing. If the person has experienced a withdrawal syndrome in the past then they will have learned that it is unpleasant but can be stopped immediately by consuming the drug. Furthermore, this expectation that the withdrawal syndrome is unpleasant could actually lead to an exacerbation of the symptoms experienced, making the syndrome more severe than would otherwise be expected. As a result, this would lead to an increased motivation and likelihood of the person deciding to seek out more of the drug.

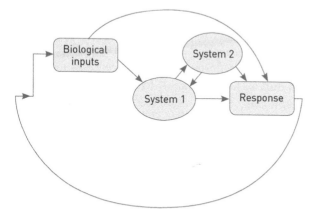

Figure 8.1 Biological inputs in the dual systems model of addictive behaviour

As another example, let's look at the increased heart rate that results from consuming a psychostimulant drug. While the increase in heart rate is a direct biological response to the action of the drug in the central and peripheral nervous systems, people are able to detect changes in their heart rate, and therefore this form of biological input will also lead to a response from the cognitive processing system. For instance, an individual who experiences a rapid increase in heart rate may interpret this as a good sign if they have regularly used the drug in the past – this might be a simple automatic association, generated as a result of frequent experiences in the past. On the other hand, a naive user of the same drug, experiencing a similar increase in heart rate, may begin to panic that something is wrong and seek advice or support.

Psycho-behavioural factors

The next category of factors that can be used to understand addictive behaviour are what we have termed *psycho-behavioural inputs*. This term is used to signify both psychological inputs, such as emotions and mood states, as well as behaviours that an individual engages in which have psychological significance, such as observing oneself injecting a drug, entering an environment normally associated with the addictive behaviour (for example a nightclub or casino), being with other people who are taking drugs, other conditioned stimuli and so forth. Figure 8.2 shows how this class of inputs can affect responses.

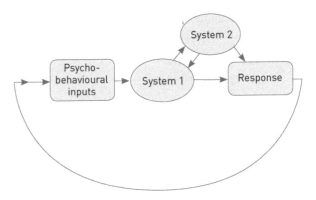

Figure 8.2 Psycho-behavioural inputs in the dual systems model of addictive behaviour

An important point to note here is that psycho-behavioural inputs cannot, by their very nature, have direct effects on responses in the absence of any cognitive processing of them. For instance, a drug-dependent individual who is in a depressed or anxious mood may or may not decide to administer their drug in order to deal with their mood. The key point here is that the effect of their mood is determined entirely by the outputs of their cognitive response to this feeling. If the individual has routinely used drugs to medicate their mood, then the response to their depressed state may automatically (that is, via System 1) be to use their drug.

On the other hand, the individual may presently be attempting to abstain from drug taking, and through the course of therapy they may have been given advice on how to deal with situations such as this, where they would ordinarily have used drugs. The individual may then engage in more effortful (that is, System 2) thinking to develop a strategy for dealing with their feelings, while also avoiding drug use.

◉ Socio-environmental factors

Finally we come to socio-environmental inputs which, like biological inputs, are also capable of directly affecting responses in the absence of any cognitive mediation. Socio-environmental inputs are taken to represent the class of influences on our behaviour that extend outside of the individual, and may include the influence of other people, social circumstances such as homelessness, or the availability and accessibility of certain drugs (for example pub opening hours, availability of illicit heroin, access to a casino and so forth). Figure 8.3 shows this class of input in our framework.

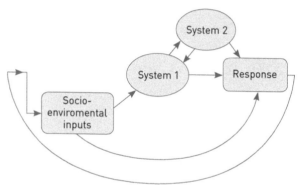

Figure 8.3 Socio-environmental inputs in the dual systems model of addictive behaviour

An example of a socio-environmental input that directly affects a response in the context of addictive behaviour would be a lack of funds for gambling. If a problem gambler found themselves being refused credit in a casino, with absolutely no other way of obtaining funds to continue gambling, then their response (that is, not gambling any more at that time) would be wholly determined by this environmental input (lacking funds to gamble with). Alternatively, another type of socio-environmental input for our problem gambler could be an appeal from their family and friends to quit gambling. This is clearly not a factor that could directly alter the individual's response, because of course they could choose to ignore this request entirely and continue gambling. Their response will once more be reliant upon the decision made as a result of processing the request made by their concerned family and friends, and this decision is made via Systems 1 and 2.

👁 An integrated framework for addictive behaviour

We now have all the constituent parts to form a completed integrated framework for understanding addictive behaviours. This framework is presented in Figure 8.4, and includes the three categories of input described above.

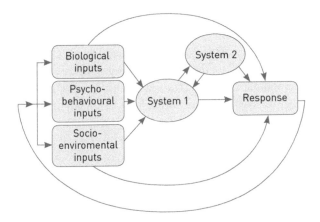

Figure 8.4 Putting it all together: A dual systems model of addictive behaviour

The model presented above shows that addictive behaviour is produced by, and maintained by, biopsychosocial factors that either have a direct effect on addictive behaviour, or are mediated by cognitive processing. Such a model incorporates many of the current theories of the aetiology and progression of addictive behaviour that we have discussed in this book. The flow chart presented can be used to describe responses that have developed over time (for example the experience of withdrawal signs and symptoms after the chronic use of a drug), as well as describing responses that will occur during (for example) a single drug-taking session. To prevent harms to the individual and community arising from an addictive behaviour we are then presented with a number of possible targets. We can remove a particular biological or socio-environmental input, and we can attempt to change System 1 (uncon-scious and automatic information processing) or strengthen System 2 (controlled and conscious information processing) cognitive processes so that they exert more of an effect on System 1. An important function of our model is to provide a clear means for mapping the various factors associated with addictive behaviours and their harms. This then provides us with a new tool for determining the most appropriate intervention or prevention strategy.

In the final part of our book, we will describe how our model explains a behaviour that is associated with significant social harm – drink-driving – and consider what the model says about strategies for reducing the prevalence of this behaviour. We have chosen this example as it is representative of the many 'indirect' harms of addictive behaviour. That is, as we have discussed throughout this book, addictive behaviour is a problem for more reasons than that it impacts negatively on those engaged in it. On the contrary, the impacts on society in the form of criminal justice costs, healthcare costs and economic costs are significant. Despite this, of the models and theories that we have discussed throughout, few if any are able to even begin speaking to these broader social issues.

Drink-driving

The number of road fatalities related to the presence of alcohol in drivers has been relatively constant over the past 10 years, despite an overall reduction in drink-driver casualties and accidents. Approximately 16 per cent of fatal car accidents in Great Britain involve drivers who test positive for the consumption of alcohol over the legal limit of 0.08 per cent (Department of Transport, 2007). Furthermore, it has been estimated that 80 road deaths every year are caused by drivers who are under the legal drink-drive limit, but who have a significant amount of alcohol in their blood (Institute of Alcohol Studies, 2004). The proportion of drivers who were killed when alcohol was present in their blood but were not over the legal limit is highest in the age brackets of people aged 20–24 and 25–29 years old (Department for Transport, 2007). This evidence suggests that people under the age of 25 are overrepresented in road collisions.

The basic concepts of driving are relatively easy to learn (Evans, 1991). However, the complex interactions of the skills required to drive a vehicle, as well as anticipation of other drivers on the road, make driving a complicated task. There is no evidence of a threshold effect of alcohol, as impairment can be seen even at the lowest concentrations (Ogden and Moskowitz, 2004). Driving-related skills that are affected by alcohol include attention and information processing, vigilance, visual function, ability to judge distance, and motor skills such as steering and braking. Ideally, we would like a situation where no one would consume alcohol and then drive a motor vehicle; however, this is not always a realistic proposition.

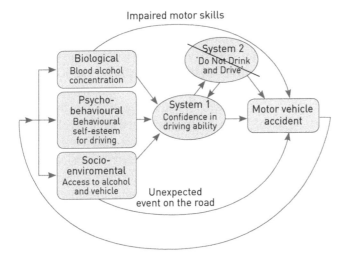

Figure 8.5 A dual systems model of addictive behaviour applied to drink-driving

In Figure 8.5 we have described some of the biopsychosocial antecedents of a motor vehicle accident (the response) that occurs after someone has been drinking alcohol. Let's look at each of the inputs in turn, beginning with the biological input.

As we showed in Chapter 2, alcohol is a central nervous system depressant that impairs our cognitive and motor skills as the blood concentration increases. In our model, increasing blood alcohol concentration will impair cognitive and motor skills to the extent that the likelihood of being involved in a motor vehicle accident increases dramatically. However, high concentrations of alcohol can also increase our confidence; and in this example, the System 1 cognitive processing will lead to increased confidence in one's ability to drive a car, especially if one is an experienced driver. Put simply, if one does not tend to associate driving a car with having an accident (which would be the case for most drivers, most of the time), then there would not necessarily be any automatic output from System 1 which might discourage drink-driving. This would only occur if the individual had previously learned to associate drink-driving with a significant likelihood of a negative outcome (that is, having an accident). In the absence of such prior learning, the individual may be significantly more likely to drink and drive if other motivating factors, discussed below, were present. On the other hand, the controlled System 2 processing that would normally tell us 'don't drink and drive' is impaired by a high blood alcohol concentration. As a result, it will not counterbalance the incorrect System 1 processing (which either is actively encouraging, or simply not discouraging the act of drinking and driving), and the person will drive and then potentially have an accident.

Obviously the amount of alcohol that one can consume, and the opportunity to drive a car, will be determined by how easy it is to access alcohol and a car. As such, the socio-environmental input is the easy access to both a car and alcohol. As we stated earlier, reaction time and visual function are some of the skills that are degraded with rising blood alcohol concentration. As a result, a driver's ability to react appropriately to an unexpected event (such as a traffic light turning to red) becomes quite impaired and a car accident can result. Furthermore, if the person is sold alcohol while obviously intoxicated, and with friends who want the person to drive, then that person's confidence in their own ability to drive (System 1) will be increased.

Finally, the person may feel that they are a good driver. Indeed, they may never have previously been involved in an accident. Being able to drive a car may also be important to their view of themselves, that is, they may have high behavioural self-esteem for driving. As a result, they may underestimate the impairment produced by drinking alcohol and overestimate their perceived skill in driving. As a result, this psycho-behavioural input will increase their confidence in their driving ability (System 1) and as a result, they may have a motor vehicle accident.

Each of these inputs, however, gives us some ideas for how we could have prevented this situation. In terms of cognitive processing, we need to focus on strengthening the cognitive association that it is never appropriate to drive a car after consuming alcohol. If this message were to begin at a very early age, before the person was legally able to drive a car, then this association may build up within System 1 as an automatic response to the act of drinking and driving – that is, the individual may begin automatically associating this behaviour with negative outcomes. If System 1 were 'trained' in this way, it would be more likely to guide behaviour when intoxicated, even if controlled processes had been weakened.

In terms of the biological input (blood alcohol concentration), we could ensure that alcohol with a lower alcohol content was cheaper and more readily available, than higher strength alcohol. We could also serve alcohol in such a way as to slow the rate of increase in blood alcohol concentration, such as by ensuring that food is readily available and that people do not drink alcohol too quickly (both techniques would slow the rate of ethanol absorption). Similarly, we can ensure our pubs and other venues make it easier for people to avoid drinking alcohol, for example by serving non-alcoholic drinks, or closing the bar well before closing the establishment. If people do persist in driving after drinking, then we could try to ensure that the likelihood that they will be intercepted by the police is increased by funding random breath-alcohol and impairment tests on drivers.

In terms of the socio-environmental inputs, our first step may be to train bar staff not to serve alcohol to people who are intoxicated. Similarly, we can ensure that there is cheap and frequent public transport available to provide a viable alternative to driving a car. Finally, we can target the psycho-behavioural input by ensuring that our prevention programmes focus on building the view that self-esteem can be enhanced by driving safely.

◉ Summary and concluding remarks

In this chapter we have presented a framework for understanding addictive behaviours that incorporates evidence and ideas from a very wide range of disciplines. Our intention in developing this new model is to provide a simplified way of conceptualizing the complex nature of addictive behaviours, based upon the evidence presented throughout this text. We have also given an overview of how this model might be applied to understand not only the causes of addictive behaviours, but also how the model can help to identify ways of preventing behaviours such as this. What this shows is that, once you are able to appreciate the kinds of factors that can influence risky or otherwise unhealthy behaviours, including biological as well as psychological and social influences, it becomes easier to identify ways of intervening in and preventing the behaviour itself.

What we have also shown throughout this book is that many areas of research in the field of addictions have grown up in relative isolation from one another – this does not have to be the case. Biological and psychopharmacological research, for example, provides much understanding of the processes involved in the development of addictive behaviours, but the knowledge gained in this area, once interpreted in light of broader theories of human behaviour, begins to contribute far more to an overall understanding of addictive behaviour.

We believe that this is an exciting time in addictive behaviour research, and treatment and prevention development. Advances in our ability to see inside the brain, even down to the level of the individual receptor, in the field of neuroimaging are shedding greater light on the mechanisms of addictive behaviours, and the structures and processes of the brain that underpin this behaviour. The growth in psychopharmacology (the study of drugs on cognition and behaviour) demonstrates the power of interdisciplinary collaboration and knowledge exchange in understanding biopsychosocial phenomena like addictive behaviour. Progress in these areas is paralleled by advances in mainstream cognitive science and psychology that are providing us with new ways of understanding some of the most fundamental questions about human existence, such as the nature of consciousness and free will. The research we discussed in this book's later chapters, which shows an increase in the application of these mainstream cognitive science and psychological theories, is an extremely encouraging sign of progress in this field.

Psychology and psychopharmacology have a lot to offer in our understanding of addictive behaviour, and, through developing our understanding of this disorder, these fields are shedding greater light on issues such as self-control and choice, which have relevance to our understanding of ourselves.

◉ Further reading

Moss, A.C. and Albery, I.P. (2009) A dual-process model of the alcohol–behavior link for social drinking. *Psychological Bulletin*, 135, 516–30.

Evans, St. B.T. and Frankish, K. (2009) *In Two Minds: Dual Processes and Beyond*. Oxford: Oxford University Press.

Glossary

Absorption the process by which a drug enters the blood stream.

Abstinence violation effect the effects and consequences of failing to remain abstinent, which can lead to an individual experiencing strong negative emotions around their failure.

Action potential the electrical message that travels along a neuron to transfer information and trigger the release of neurotransmitters at the synapse.

Agonist drugs that bind to a receptor and activate the neuron.

Antagonist drugs that bind to a receptor but do not activate the neuron, which also prevent agonists from activating the neuron.

Attentional bias the phenomenon whereby individuals tend to be distracted by objects and stimuli that have some personal relevance to them. Attentional biases for drug and alcohol-related stimuli have been shown to increase as a function of past use, and become particularly strong among dependent users.

Automatic cognitive process automatic cognitive processes are directly activated by the presence of certain stimuli, they are 'ballistic' and very difficult, if not impossible, to interrupt once active. They consume hardly any attentional resources, and they are able to run in parallel with many other processes (including **controlled cognitive processes**).

Automaticity behaviours that occur without the need for conscious control or monitoring are said to occur automatically. Automaticity refers to this general ability, and can include both simple and complex social behaviours.

Behaviourist theory *see* **Learning theory**

Blood–brain barrier a protective barrier between the brain and the blood stream which prevents many but not all toxins from passing from the blood stream into the brain. Most drugs of dependence have the effects that they do because they are able to pass this barrier.

Cellular tolerance (also *pharmacodynamic tolerance*) tolerance to the effects of a drug, which is caused by physical alterations in brain function.

Classical conditioning (also *Pavlovian conditioning*) learning through association, so that stimuli in our environment can become associated with previously unrelated outcomes.

Cognitive behavioural therapy treatment that involves trying to understand dysfunctional ways of thinking, and to identify environmental triggers that lead to craving and/or engagement in addictive behaviour.

Cognitive decoupling decoupling is the ability to think about the world in ways *which it is not*. This is also sometimes referred to as hypothetical thinking, and allows us, for example, to predict the outcomes of different actions on the world around us, without the need for actually engaging in each action.

Cognitive miser describes the general observation that people tend to rely on mental shortcuts whenever possible, rather than fully evaluating all new information that is encountered. An example of cognitive miserliness is the use of stereotypes to categorize other people and to make judgements about the causes of their behaviour.

Conditioned tolerance and withdrawal tolerance and withdrawal when they occur independently of pharmacological causes. Conditioned tolerance and withdrawal can occur many months or even years after an individual has ceased drug or alcohol use.

Contiguity an important condition for learning to occur effectively, such that we learn better when our actions and their consequences occur in closer proximity in time.

Controlled cognitive process controlled cognitive processes are characterized as being fairly slow (compared to **automatic cognitive processes**) and dependent on attentional capacity. They are not context or stimulus dependent, and they operate serially to one another.

Craving the strong subjective desire to want to use a drug or engage in an addictive behaviour. Craving can be physiologically (that is, as a result of physical withdrawal symptoms) and/or psychologically (that is, as a result of learned responses to drug-related triggers or cues) motivated.

Cross-tolerance if tolerance develops to a specific drug, then tolerance will also be developed to all drugs within the same drug class.

Delirium tremens a condition related to alcohol withdrawal syndrome that includes confusion, agitation and aggression. Also known as the 'DTs' or 'the shakes', delirium tremens (from the Latin 'shaking delirium') often includes uncontrollable tremors.

Detoxification a medical intervention for drug dependence, which involves giving decreasing doses of the drug, or administering a replacement drug that has similar effects to the drug of dependence.

Distribution the process by which a drug reaches the brain and other parts of the body, after it has been absorbed in to the blood stream.

Drug a chemical substance, with a known chemical structure that produces a biological and psychological effect when it is administered.

Drug liking in the context of incentive-sensitization theory, drug liking refers to the subjective desire for a drug, in order to obtain some positive effects from it (whether that is to achieve a euphoric mood, or to eliminate withdrawal symptoms).

Drug wanting in the context of incentive-sensitization theory, drug wanting refers to the impulse to use a drug, which is independent of any conscious desire based upon anticipated positive outcomes.

Dual systems theory (also *dual process theory*) dual systems theories of human thinking posit that the basic architecture of the human mind contains two components: a fast, efficient and often unconscious component (see **System 1** and **automatic cognitive process**) and a slower, resource-intensive and conscious component (see **System 2** and **controlled cognitive process**).

Energy model of self-regulation a model of self-control that posits that one's ability to exercise conscious self-control is a limited resource that can be exhausted in the short term. As a result, engaging in acts of effortful self-control can reduce one's ability to exercise self-control in other instances immediately afterwards.

Epistemic rationality a form of rationality that means an individual actively seeks to ensure that the knowledge, beliefs and goals they possess actually reflect reality. Individuals who do not demonstrate this form of rationality will show tendencies to retain beliefs even when evidence is presented that disconfirms them, even when a change in their beliefs would be advantageous to the individual.

Excretion the elimination from the body of a drug and its metabolites.

Expectancies beliefs about the likely outcomes of actions that are built up over an individual's lifetime, as a result of their direct and indirect learning experiences.

Expectancy-value the extent to which we desire, or not, a particular outcome of an action.

Half-life the amount of time taken for half of the amount of a drug to be eliminated from the body. Drugs with longer half-lives will have longer lasting effects on the individual, while drugs with shorter half-lives will need to be re-administered in shorter intervals to avoid experiencing withdrawal symptoms.

Health economics that branch of economics, sometimes called *medical economics*, which is concerned with the full economic costs of illnesses and interventions. When assessing the effectiveness of an intervention for treating a particular illness or disease, health economists consider the broader implications and effects on the treatment, beyond simply how well it addresses the illness itself, including additional benefits to the individual and society.

Heuristic a heuristic is a simple mental shortcut or 'rule of thumb' that allows us to make decisions or judgements quickly and efficiently. Heuristics usually develop as a result of past learning experiences, although some may be innately specified.

Homeostasis the physiological process by which bodily systems are maintained at a steady state of equilibrium.

Incentive salience this is said to occur when an object or cue becomes associated with a positive reward, and so is something that will be evaluated favourably in future.

Incentive-sensitization theory a theory of addictive behaviour that has been used to explain the development of compulsive drug use and drug urges. The theory also provides an explanation for why drug dependence persists even when an individual has decided they would prefer to stop using.

Inhibitory control the general ability to suppress a behavioural response, which is linked with the anterior cingulate and orbitofrontal cortices in the brain. Damage to these brain regions, which can happen as a result of long-term drug use, can lead to individuals becoming more impulsive and less able to suppress drug-use behaviours.

Inhibitory dysregulation a theory of the addictive behaviour that posits that long-term drug use leads to a reduction in inhibitory control, hence individuals become less able to control drug-use behaviours.

Instrumental rationality a form of rationality which means that an individual will seek to act in ways that help them to effectively achieve their goals. Individuals who do not demonstrate this form of rationality will behave in ways that are counterproductive, and do not help them to achieve their own goals effectively.

Learning theory (also *behaviourist theory*) a theoretical framework in psychology that explains behaviour as the result of learned stimulus–response relationships. Learning theorists traditionally exclude unobservable mentalistic concepts such as motivation and desire from their explanations of behaviour and learning.

Metabolic tolerance (also *pharmacokinetic tolerance*) tolerance to a drug that occurs because the body becomes increasingly efficient at eliminating the drug over time and repeated use.

Metabolism the process through which the body breaks down a drug into derivative chemicals that are more easily excreted from the body.

Modelling (also *vicarious learning*) learning that occurs through observation of others. This means that we can learn through the experience of others' punishments and rewards to determine whether or not we should imitate their behaviour.

Monoamines a class of neurotransmitters that are associated with cognitive function, emotions and behaviour.

Motivational interviewing a form of counselling that involves helping the person to make a decision to change their drug use while at the same time accepting the responsibility of that decision. At its most basic, it involves exploring the good things and less good things about drug use, and building upon any concerns of drug use.

Mucous membrane tissue layers in the body that are highly absorbent, including the lining of the nose, lungs and mouth. A number of routes of drug administration, such as smoking (for example tobacco, cannabis) and snorting (for example cocaine), exploit the fact that mucous membranes are much more absorbent than the skin, and therefore allow chemicals to enter the blood stream.

Needle freaking a form of drug-like conditioned response where it has been observed that heroin-dependent patients will exhibit signs of having injected heroin, when in fact they have knowingly only injected a saline solution into themselves. It is thought that the simple act of injecting oneself, which has been continuously associated with actual drug use in the past, causes this response.

Negative reinforcement a consequence of an action that leads to relief from some negative state, and subsequently increases the future likelihood of that action when the negative state is experienced again (for example taking a drug to alleviate negative withdrawal symptoms).

Neuroadaptation physical and chemical changes that occur in the brain as a result of repeated drug use over time, and are associated with tolerance and the appearance of the withdrawal syndrome. Neuroadaptation can be thought of as representing the body's attempt to minimize the impact of a drug.

Neurons specialized cells in the body that allow for information transfer throughout the nervous system.

Neurotransmission the process by which information is passed from one neuron to another, via the synapse.

Neurotransmitter chemicals in the brain, which are released by neurons at the synapse, which can bind to the receptors on another neuron, which can then trigger another action potential in this neuron, thereby carrying the message across neurons and throughout the nervous system.

Operant conditioning learning which occurs through consequences that either reward or punish behaviour to increase or decrease, respectively, the likelihood of the behaviour occurring again in future.

Opioids a generic term applied to derivatives obtained from the opium poppy (*Papaver somniferum*), their synthetic analogues and compounds produced within the body. All these substances interact with specific opioid receptors in the brain, and can relieve pain and produce a sense of wellbeing.

Peer support programmes peer support programmes (also known as self help groups) offer ongoing social support to people who are attempting to stop drug use. They are offered by people who have themselves previously experienced drug problems.

Pharmacodynamic tolerance *see* **Cellular tolerance**

Pharmacokinetic tolerance *see* **Metabolic tolerance**

Physical dependence the state where tolerance to a drug has been developed, and a physical withdrawal syndrome will occur during periods of abstinence.

Physical withdrawal syndrome when an individual stops using a drug, they may experience depression, nausea or flu-like symptoms. This is known as a physical withdrawal syndrome.

Positive reinforcement a consequence of an action that leads to a pleasurable experience, which subsequently increases the future likelihood of that action in order to obtain the desired pleasurable stimulus (for example taking a drug and experiencing a pleasurable, euphoric mental state).

Prevention refers to initiatives and interventions that are aimed at preventing addictive behaviours from developing in the first place.

Primary prevention interventions that target individuals who have not yet begun using alcohol and other drugs, or started gambling and so forth. Their goal is to challenge the individual and/or environmental factors that promote unhealthy behaviour.

Protection adoption process model (PAPM) a stage theory of health behaviour change, which specifies the stages through which a person must pass in order to change their behaviour, from ignorance of the health issue to having successfully changed behaviour.

Psychological dependence a compulsion to engage in an addictive behaviour that can persist for a long period of time after the addictive behaviour has stopped.

Psychostimulants drugs that stimulate the central nervous system include caffeine, cocaine (cocaine hydrochloride), crack (cocaine base), amphetamine, methamphetamine and ecstasy (MDMA: methyl-dioxy-methamphetamine). Using a psychostimulant will produce symptoms that include arousal, reduced fatigue, euphoria, positive mood, accelerated heart rate, elevated blood pressure, pupil dilation, increased temperature, reduced appetite, and short-term improvement in cognitive domains including sustained attention.

Punishment a negative, aversive consequence of an action, which subsequently leads to a decreased likelihood of the action being performed in future (for example experiencing nausea and vomiting if alcohol is consumed while taking Antabuse (disulfiram)).

Rational thoughts and behaviours are usually described as being rational when they are in some sense optimal. That is, the behaviour or thought is the most efficient way of achieving a given goal or objective.

Receptors receptors are protein molecules that recognize and respond to endogenous chemical compounds called neurotransmitters, which send messages between the cells in the brain.

Reciprocal determinism the idea that individuals are both affected by and have effects upon their environment. This principle was adopted in social learning theory.

Reward pathway the region of the brain that is involved in learning, and produces emotional responses.

Routes of administration a route of administration in the context of drug use is the path by which a drug is taken into the body. For drugs of abuse, common routes of administration include oral (via mouth), intranasal (via nose), injecting into a muscle or vein or applying to the skin.

Schema (plural: schemata) a schema is a complex framework of interconnected information in memory that represents some aspect of the world. These 'aspects' could range from specific action scripts (for example how to make a cup of tea), to the way in which you think about yourself (a self-schema). Schemata can be thought of as complex forms of mental **heuristics** in that they represent a way of using previous knowledge of the world to help predict future ways of thinking, behaving or assimilating new information.

Secondary prevention strategies that involve screening and detecting drug use and other addictive behaviours at an early stage in order to intervene before significant problems have developed.

Self-efficacy beliefs held by an individual about their ability to carry out an action. Self-efficacy is an important concept in psychology as high or low self-efficacy can predict the likelihood that an individual will attempt, and be successful in, carrying out a particular action.

Social learning theory a theoretical model for explaining human behaviour that extended the earlier learning theory to include cognitive mediation of information in explanations of behaviour.

States personality characteristics that are highly time and situation dependent.

Syllogistic reasoning syllogistic reasoning involves deciding whether a given conclusion is true if two premises are taken to be true. In a syllogistic reasoning task, one is asked to decide whether, if two given premises are true, the conclusion *has* to be true (see example in Chapter 5).

Synapse the gap between neurons across which neurotransmitters must pass in order to carry a signal from one neuron to another.

System 1 the automatic cognitive processing system which is fast, does not require conscious control or monitoring to operate, and is evolutionarily the earliest system.

System 2 the controlled cognitive processing system which is (relatively) slow, requires conscious control and monitoring to operate, and is an evolutionarily recent system.

Tertiary prevention designed to prevent addictive behaviours developing further, and to minimize the likelihood of serious medical and psychosocial consequences associated with drug dependence.

Tolerance the diminishing effect of the same dose of a drug after repeated use, such that larger doses are required to achieve the original effects of the smaller dose.

Traits personality characteristics that vary little over time or across situations.

Trait theories of personality explanations of human personality that posit that personality is composed of several underlying traits, or characteristics, which tend not to change greatly over time. Different theorists have suggested varying numbers of these core traits, which can include characteristics such as extraversion, conscientiousness, and openness.

Transporter neurotransmitter transporters are protein molecules that carry a neurotransmitter across cell membranes or remove neurotransmitters from the synaptic cleft, ending their action. Occasionally, transporters can work in reverse, transporting neurotransmitters into the synapse, allowing these neurotransmitters to bind to their receptors and exert their effect.

References

Ajzen, I. (1991) The theory of planned behaviour. *Organizational Behavior and Human Decision Processes*, 50, 179–211.

American Psychiatric Association (2000) *Diagnostic and Statistical Manual of Mental Disorders* (4th edn) *Text Revision*. Washington, DC: American Psychiatric Association.

Anderson, P., Chisholm, D. and Fuhr, D. (2009) Effectiveness and cost-effectiveness of policies and programmes to reduce the harm caused by alcohol. *The Lancet*, 373, 2234–46.

Andrews, P.W. and Thomson, J.A. Jr. (2009) The bright side of being blue: Depression as an adaptation for analyzing complex problems. *Psychological Review*, 116, 620–54.

Baer, J.S. (1993) Etiology and secondary prevention of alcohol problems with young adults. In J.S. Baer, G.A. Marlatt and R.J. MacMahon (eds) *Addictive Behaviors Across the Lifespan*, Newbury Park, CA: Sage.

Bandura, A. (1977) *Social Learning Theory*. Englewood Cliffs, NJ: Prentice-Hall.

Bargh, J.A., Chen, M. and Burrows, L. (1996) Automaticity of social behaviour: Direct effects of trait construct and stereotype activation on action. *Journal of Personality and Social Psychology*, 71, 230–44.

Baumeister, R.F. (2003) Ego depletion and self-regulation failure: A resource model of self-control. *Alcoholism: Clinical and Experimental Research*, 27, 1–4.

Becker, G.S. and Murphy. K.M. (1988) A theory of rational addiction. *Journal of Political Economy*, 96, 675–700.

Beevers, C.G. (2005) Cognitive vulnerability to depression: A dual process model. *Clinical Psychology Review*, 25, 975–1002.

Begg, E. (2001) *Clinical Pharmacology Essentials* (2nd edn). Auckland: ADIS International.

Brewer, J.A. and Potenza, M.N. (2008) The neurobiology and genetics of impulse control disorder: Relationships to drug addictions. *Biochemical Pharmacology*, 75, 63–75.

Bühringer, G. and Pfeiffer-Gerschel, T. (2008) Combine and match: The final blow for large-scale black box randomized controlled trials. *Addiction*, 103, 708–10.

Burns, M.O. and Seligman, M.E.P. (1989) Explanatory style across the life span: Evidence for stability over 52 years. *Journal of Personality and Social Psychology*, 56, 471–7.

Cattell, R.B. (1957) *Personality and Motivation Structure and Measurement*. New York: World Book.

Christiansen, B.A., Smith, G.T., Roehling, P.V. and Goldman, M.S. (1989) Using alcohol expectancies to predict adolescent drinking behaviour after one year. *Journal of Consulting and Clinical Psychology*, 57, 93–9.

Cloninger, C.R. (1987) A systematic method for clinical description and classification of personality variants. *Archives of General Psychiatry*, 44, 573–88.

The COMBINE Study Research Group (2003) Testing combined pharmacotherapies and behavioral interventions in alcohol dependence: Rationale and methods. *Alcoholism: Clinical & Experimental Research*, 27, 1107–22.

Cox, W.M., Fadardi, J.S. and Pothos, E.M. (2006) The Addiction-Stroop Test: Theoretical considerations and procedural recommendations. *Psychological Bulletin*, 132, 443–76.

Cruickshank, C. and Dyer, K.R. (2009) A review of the clinical pharmacology of methamphetamine. *Addiction*, 104, 1085–99.

Cruickshank, C., Montebello, M., Dyer, K.R., Quigley, A., Blaszczyk, J., Tomkins, S. and Shand, D. (2008) A placebo-controlled trial of mirtazapine for the management of methamphetamine withdrawal. *Drug & Alcohol Review*, 27(3): 326–33.

Cutler, R.B. and Fishbain, D.A. (2005) Are alcoholism treatments effective? The Project MATCH data. *BMC Public Health*, 5, 75.

Davies, L., Jones, A., Vamvakas, G., Dubourg, R. and Donmall, M. (2009) *The Drug Treatment Outcomes Research Study (DTORS): Cost-effectiveness Analysis* (2nd edn). London: The Home Office.

De Haes, W. and Schuurman, J. (1975) Results of an evaluation study on three drug education models. *International Journal of Health Education*, 18 (Supplement).

De Haes, W. and Schuurman, J. (1987) Looking for effective drug education programmes: Exploration of the effects of different drug reduction programmes. *Health Education Research*, 2(4): 433–8.

Department for Transport (2007) *Road Casualties Great Britain: 2007: Annual Report*. London, Transport Statistics. [Online] Available at: http://www.dft.gov.uk/pgr/statistics/datatablepublications/accidents/casualtiesgbar/ [Accessed 10 November 2008]

DiClemente, C.C. and Prochaska, J.O. (1982) Self-change and therapy change of smoking behavior: A comparison of processes of change in cessation and maintenance. *Addictive Behaviors*, 7, 133–42.

DiClemente, C.C., Prochaska, J.O. and Gibertini, M. (1985) Self-efficacy and the stages of self-change of smoking. *Cognitive Therapy and Research*, 9, 181–200.

Dijksterhuis, A. and van Knippenberg, A. (1998) The relation between perception and behaviour or how to win a game of Trivial Pursuit. *Journal of Personality and Social Psychology*, 74, 865–77.

Doll, R. and Hill, A.B. (1950) Smoking and carcinoma of the lung; preliminary report. *British Medical Journal*, 4682, 739–48.

Doran, C., Vos, T., Cobiac, L., Hall, W., Asamoah, I., Wallace, A. et al. (2008) Identifying cost-effective interventions to reduce the burden of harm associated with alcohol misuse in Australia. University of Queensland. Retrieved 4 August 2009 from http://www.aerf.com.au/showcase/MediaReleases/2008/Doran%20 AERF%20report.pdf.

Downs, C. and Woolrych, R. (October 2009) *Gambling and Debt Pathfinder Study*. Manchester Metropolitan University: Research Institute for Health and Social Change.

Dunn, M.E. and Goldman, M.S. (1996) Empirical modelling of an alcohol expectancy memory network in elementary school children as a function of grade. *Experimental and Clinical Psychopharmacology*, 4, 209–17.

Dunn, M.E. and Goldman, M.S. (1998) Age and drinking-related differences in the memory organization of alcohol expectancies in

3rd-, 6th-, 9th- and 12th-grade children. *Journal of Consulting and Clinical Psychology*, 66, 579–85.

Dyer, K.R. and Cruickshank, C. (2005) Depression and other psychological health problems among methamphetamine dependent patients in treatment: Implications for assessment and treatment outcome. *Australian Psychologist* 40(2): 96–108.

Dyer, K.R. and Wilkinson, C. (2008) The detection of illicit drugs in oral fluid: A potential strategy to reduce illicit drug-related harm. *Drug & Alcohol Review*, 27(1): 99–107.

Ehrman, R.N., Ternes, J.T., O'Brien, C.P. and McLellan, A.T. (1992) Conditioned tolerance in human opiate addicts. *Psychopharmacology*, 108, 218–24.

Evans, L. (1991) *Traffic Safety and the Driver*. New York, Van Norstrand Reinhold E.J.

Eysenck, H.J. and Eysenck, M.W. (1985) *Personality and Individual Differences: A Natural Science Approach*. New York: Plenum.

Fadardi, J.S. and Cox, W.M. (2009) Reversing the sequence: Reducing alcohol consumption by overcoming alcohol attentional bias. *Drug and Alcohol Dependence*, 101, 137–45.

Faggiano, F. and EU-DAP Study Group (2010) The effectiveness of a school-based substance abuse prevention programme: 18 month follow-up of the EU-DAP cluster randomised controlled trial. *Drug and Alcohol Dependence*, 108, 56–64.

Field, M., Munafò, M.R. and Franken, I.H.A. (2009) A meta-analytic investigation of the relationship between attentional bias and subjective craving in substance abuse. *Psychological Bulletin*, 135, 589–607.

Field, M. and Cox, W.M. (2008) Attentional bias in addictive behaviors: A review of its development, causes and consequences. *Drug and Alcohol Dependence*, 97, 1–20.

Field, M., Duka, T., Eastwood, B., Child, R., Santarcangelo, M. and Gayton, M. (2007) Experimental manipulation of attentional biases in heavy drinkers: Do the effects generalise? *Psychopharmacology*, 192, 593–608.

Field, M., Duka,T., Tyler, E. and Schoenmakers, T. (2009) Attentional bias modification in tobacco smokers. *Nicotine & Tobacco Research*, 11, 812–22.

Fishbein, M. and Ajzen, I. (1975) *Belief, Attitude, Intention and Behavior: An Introduction to Theory and Research*. Reading, MA: Addison-Wesley.

Flay, B. and Sobel, J. (1983) The role of mass media in preventing adolescent substance abuse. NIDA Research Monograph 47 In T. Glynn, C. Leukefeld and J. Ludford (eds) *Preventing Adolescent Drug Abuse: Intervention Strategies.* Rockville, MD: National Institute for Drug Abuse (pp. 5–35).

Fontana, D.J., Post, R.M. and Pert, A. (1993) Conditioned increases in mesolimbic dopamine overflow by stimuli associated with cocaine. *Brain Research*, 629, 31–9.

Franken, I.H.A. (2003) Drug craving and addiction: Integrating psychological and neuropsychopharmacological approaches. *Progress in Neuro-Psychopharmacology and Biological Psychiatry*, 27, 563–79.

Frankfurt, H.G. (1971) Freedom of the will and the concept of a person. *Journal of Philosophy*, 68, 5–20.

Friese, M., Bargas-Avila, J., Hofmann, W. and Wiers, R.W. (2010) Here's looking at you, Bud: Alcohol-related memory structures predict eye movements for social drinkers with low executive control. *Social Psychological and Personality Science*, 1, 143–51.

Gailliot, M.T. and Baumeister, R.F. (2007) The physiology of willpower: Linking blood glucose to self-control. *Personality and Social Psychology Review*, 11, 303–27.

Gailliot, M.T., Baumeister, R.F., DeWall, C.N., Maner, J.K., Plant, E.A., Tice, D.M., Brewer, L.E. and Schmeichel, B.J. (2007) Self-control relies on glucose as a limited energy source: Willpower is more than a metaphor. *Journal of Personality and Social Psychology*, 92, 325–36.

Gerrard, M., Gibbons, F.X., Houlihan, A.E., Stock M.L. and Pomery, E.A. (2008) A dual-process approach to health risk decision making: The prototype willingness model. *Developmental Review*, 28, 29–61.

Godin, G. and Kok, G. (1996) The theory of planned behavior: A review of its applications to health-related behaviors. *American Journal of Health Promotion*, 11, 87–98.

Goethals, G.R. and Reckman, R.F. (1973) The perception of consistency in attitudes. *Journal of Experimental Social Psychology*, 9, 491–501.

Gossop, M., Marsden, J., Stewart, D. and Kidd, T. (2003) The National Treatment Outcome Research Study (NTORS): 4–5 year follow-up results. *Addiction*, 98, 291–303.

Gossop, M., Marsden, J., Stewart, D., and Treacy, S. (2001) Outcomes after methadone maintenance and methadonereduction treatments:

Two-year follow-up results from the National Treatment Outcome Research Study. *Drug and Alcohol Dependence*, 62, 255–64.

Gowing, L., Proudfoot, H., Henry-Edwards, S. and Teeson, M. (2001) *Evidence Supporting Treatment. The Effectiveness of Interventions for Illicit Drug Use*. ACT: Australian National Council on Drugs.

Greenberg, J., Solomon, S. and Pyszczynski, T. (1997) Terror management theory of self-esteem and cultural worldviews: Empirical assessments and. *Advances in experimental social psychology* 29(61): 139.

Houben, K. and Wiers, R.W. (2009) Response inhibition moderates the relationship between implicit associations and drinking behavior. *Alcoholism, Clinical and Experimental Research*, 33, 626–33.

Institute of Alcohol Studies (IAS) (2007) *IAS Factsheet: Drinking in Great Britain*. [Online] Available on: http://www.ias.org.uk/resources/factsheets/drinkinggb.pdf [Accessed 20 January 2009]

Jarvis, T., Tebbutt, J. and Mattick, R. (1995) *Treatment Approaches for Alcohol and Drug Dependence. An Introductory Guide*. Brisbane: John Wiley & Sons.

Jellinek, E.M. (1960) *The Disease Concept of Alcoholism*. New Brunswick, NJ: Hillhouse Press.

Jessop, D., Albery, IP., Rutter, J. and Garrod, H. (2008) Understanding the impact of mortality-related health-risk information: A terror management theory perspective. *Personality and Social Psychology Bulletin*, 34(7): 951–64.

Jones, B.T., Bruce, G., Livingstone, S. and Reed, E. (2006) Alcohol-related attentional bias in problem drinkers with the flicker change blindness paradigm. *Psychology of Addictive Behaviors*, 20, 171–7.

Jones, S. and Gregory, P. (2009) The impact of more visible standard drink labelling on youth alcohol consumption: Helping young people drink (ir)responsibly. *Drug & Alcohol Review*, 28, 230–4.

Leshner, A.I. (1997) Addiction is a brain disease and it matters. *Science*, 278(5335): 45–8.

Levine, D.G. (1974) 'Needle Freaks': Compulsive self-injection drug users. *American Journal of Psychiatry*, 131, 297–300.

Leyton, M. (2007) Conditioned and sensitized responses to stimulant drugs in humans. *Progress in Neuropsychopharmacology and Biological Psychiatry*, 31, 1601–13.

Liappas, J.A., Lascaratos, J., Fafouti, S. and Christodolou, G.N. (2003) Alexander the Great's relationship with alcohol. *Addiction*, 98, 561–7.

Lowinson, J.H., Ruiz, P. and Millman, R.B. (eds) (1992) *Substance Abuse. A Comprehensive Textbook*. Baltimore: Williams & Wilkins.

Lubman, D.I., Yücel, M. and Pantelis, C. (2004) Addiction, a condition of compulsive behaviour? Neuroimaging and neuropsychological evidence of inhibitory dysregulation. *Addiction*, 99, 1491–502.

Ludwig, A.M. (1988) *Understanding the Alcoholic's Mind. The Nature of Craving and How to Control It*. New York: Oxford University Press.

MacAndrew, C. and Edgerton, R.B. (1969) *Drunken Comportment: A Social Explanation*. Chicago: Aldine.

MacLeod, J. (2002) Excessive appetites: A psychological view of addictions (2nd edn) [book review]. *Family Practice*, 19, 118–19.

Marlatt, G.A. (1979) A cognitive-behavioral model of the relapse process. In N.A. Krasnegor (ed.), *Behavioral Analysis and Treatment of Substance Abuse: N.I.D.A. Research Monographs*, 25, Department of Health, Education and Welfare.

Marlatt, G.A. and Gordon, J.R. (eds) (1985) *Relapse Prevention: Maintenance Strategies in the Treatment of Addictive Behaviours*. New York: Guilford.

Marlatt, G.A., Baer, J.S. and Quigley, L.A. (1994) Self-efficacy and addictive behavior. In A. Bandura (ed.), *Self-efficacy in Changing Societies*. Marbach, Germany: Johann Jacobs Foundation.

Marlatt, G.A., Curry, S. and Gordon, J.R. (1988) A longitudinal analysis of unaided smoking cessation. *Journal of Consulting and Clinical Psychology*, 56, 715–20.

McCrae, R.R. and Costa, P.T. (1990) *Personality in Adulthood*. New York: The Guildford Press.

McMillan, B. and Conner, M. (2003) Applying an extended version of the theory of planned behaviour to illicit drug use amongst students. *Journal of Applied Social Psychology*, 33, 1662–83.

Melmon, K., Morrelli, H.F., Hoffman, B.B. and Nierenberg, D.W. (eds) (1992) *Clinical Pharmacoloy: Basic Principles in Therapeutics*. New York: McGraw Hill.

Miller, N.S. and Gold, M.S. (1994) Dissociation of 'conscious desire' (craving) from and relapse in alcohol and cocaine dependence, *Annals of Clinical Psychiatry*. 6, 99–106.

Moss, A.C. and Albery, I.P. (2009) A dual-process model of the alcohol–behavior link for social drinking. *Psychological Bulletin*, 135, 516–30.

Moss, A.C. and Albery, I.P. (2010) Are alcohol expectancies associations, propositions, or elephants? A reply to Wiers and Stacy (2010). *Psychological Bulletin*, 136, 17–20.

Moss, A.C., Dyer, K.R. and Albery, I. (2009) Knowledge of drinking guidelines does not guarantee sensible drinking: Evidence from London medical students. *The Lancet*, 374, 1242.

Muraven, M. and Shmueli, D. (2006) The self-control costs of fighting the temptation to drink. *Psychology of Addictive Behaviors*, 20, 154–60.

Nisbett, R. and Wilson, T. (1977) Telling more than we can know: Verbal reports on mental processes. *Psychological Review*, 84, 231–59.

O'Brien, C., Childress, A., McLellan, A. and Ehrman, R. (1992) Classical conditioning in drug-dependent humans. *Annals of the NY Academy of Sciences*, 654, 400–15.

Office for National Statistics (2008) Mortality Statistics, Deaths Registered in 2008, England and Wales. http://www.statistics.gov.uk/downloads/theme_health/DR2008/DR_08.pdf

Ogden, E.J.D. and Moskowitz, H. (2004) Effects of alcohol and other drugs on driver performance. *Traffic Injury Prevention*, 5, 185–98.

Orford, J. (2001) Addiction as excessive appetite. *Addiction*, 96, 15–31.

Orford, J. (2002) *Excessive Appetites: A Psychological View of Addictions* (2nd edn). London: John Wiley.

Post, T., van den Assem, M.J., Baltussen, G. and Thaler, R.H. (2008) Deal Or No Deal? Decision making under risk in a large-payoff game show. *American Economic Review*, 98, 1–54.

Prescott, C.A. and Kendler, K.S. (1999) Genetic and environmental contributions to alcohol abuse and dependence in a population-based sample of male twins. *American Journal of Psychiatry*, 156, 34–40.

Prochaska, J.O., Redding, C.A. and Evers, K.E. (2002) The transtheoretical model and stages of change. In K. Glanz, B.K. Rimer and K. Viswanath (eds) *Health Behavior and Health Education* (4th edn). San Francisco: Jossey-Bass (pp. 99–120).

Project MATCH Research Group (1997) Matching alcoholism treatments to client heterogeneity: Project MATCH post-treatment outcomes. *Journal of Studies on Alcohol*, 58, 7–29.

Rang, H.P., Dale, M.M., Ritter, J.M. and Flower, R.J. (2007) *Rand and Dale's Pharmacology*. Philadelphia: Churchill Livingstone Elsevier.

Reagan, A. (2009) Does the rational theory of addiction suffer explanatory impotence? In *Southern Society for Philosophy and Psychology, 101st Annual Meeting* (Savannah, GA April 9–11).

Redish, A.D. Jensen, S. and Johnson, A. (2008) A unified theory of addiction: Vulnerabilities in the decision process. *Behavioral and Brain Sciences*, 31, 415–87.

Robins, L.N. (1975) Drug treatment after return in Vietnam veterans. *Highlights of the 20th Annual Conference*, Veterans Administration Studies in Mental Health and Behavioral Sciences. Perry Point, MD: Central NP Research Laboratory.

Robinson, T.E. and Berridge, K.C. (1993) The neural basis of drug craving: An incentive-sensitization theory of addiction. *Brain Research Reviews*, 18, 247–91.

Robinson, T.E. and Berridge, K.C. (2000) The psychology and neurobiology of addiction: An incentive-sensitization view. *Addiction*, 95, 91–117.

Robinson, T.E. and Berridge, K.C. (2008) The incentive sensitization theory of addiction: Some current issues. *Philosophical Transactions of the Royal Society B*, 363, 3137–46.

Saunders, B., Wilkinson, C. and Allsop, S. (1991) Motivational interviewing intervention with heroin users attending a methadone clinic. In W.R. Miller and S. Rollnick, *Motivational Interviewing: Preparing People to Change*. New York: Guilford Press (pp. 248–85).

Schneider, W. and Chein, J.M. (2003) Controlled and automatic processing: Behavior, theory and biological mechanisms. *Cognitive Science*, 27, 525–59.

Schoenmakers, T., Wiers, R.W., Jones, B.T., Bruce, G. and Jansen, A.T.M. (2007) Attentional retraining decreases attentional bias in heavy drinkers without generalization. *Addiction*, 102, 399–405.

Schoenmakers, T.M., deBruin, M., Lux, I.F.M., Goertz, A.G., Van Kerkhof, D.H.A.T. and Wiers, R.W. (2010) Clinical effectiveness of attentional bias modification training in abstinent alcoholic patients. *Drug and Alcohol Dependence*, 109, 30–6.

Siegel, S., Hinson, R. and Krank, M. (1978) The role of predrug signals in morphine analgesic tolerance: Support for a Pavlovian conditioning model of tolerance. *Journal of Experimental Psycholology*, 4, 188–96.

Siegel, S., Hinson, R., Krank, M. and McCully, J. (1982) Heroin overdose death: Contribution of drug-associated environmental cues. *Science*, 216, 436–7.

Skinner, B.F. (1938) *The Behavior of Organisms: An Experimental Analysis.* Cambridge, Massachusetts: B.F. Skinner Foundation.

Sokoloff, L. (1973) Metabolism of ketone bodies by the brain. *Annual Reviews in Medicine*, 24, 271–80.

Stacy, A.W., Newcomb, M.D. and Bentler, P.M. (1992) Interactive and higher-order effects of social influences on drug use. *Journal of Health Social Behavior*, 33, 226–41.

Stanovich, K.E. (2004) *The Robot's Rebellion: Finding Meaning in the Age of Darwin.* Chicago: University of Chicago Press.

Stanovich, K.E. (2009) *What Intelligence Tests Miss: The Psychology of Rational Thought.* Yale: Yale University Press.

Stroop, J.R. (1935) Studies of interference in serial verbal reactions. *Journal of Experimental Psychology*, 18, 643–62.

Sutton, S. (2001) Back to the drawing board? A review of applications of the transtheoretical model to substance use. *Addiction*, 96, 175–86.

Thomsen, S.R. and Fulton, K. (2007) Adolescents' attention to responsibility messages in magazine alcohol advertisements: An eye-tracking approach. *Journal of Adolescent Health*, 41, 27–34.

Tiffany, S.T. (1990) A cognitive model of drug urges and drug-use behavior: Role of automatic and nonautomatic processes. *Psychological Review*, 97, 147–68.

Tiffany, S.T. (1999) Cognitive concepts of craving. *Alcohol Research & Health*, 23, 215–24.

Tooby, J. and Cosmides, L. (1995) Mapping the evolved functional organization of mind and brain. In M. Gazzaniga (ed.), *The Cognitive Neurosciences*. Cambridge, MA: MIT Press.

Toplak, M.E., Liu, E., Macpherson, R., Toneatto, T. and Stanovich, K.E. (2007) The reasoning skills and thinking dispositions of problem gamblers: A dual-process taxonomy, *Journal of Behavioral Decision Making*, 20, 103–24.

Tupes, E. and Christal, R. (1992) Recurrent personality factors based on trait ratings. *Journal of Personality*, 60, 225–51.

UKATT Research Team (2005) Effectiveness of treatment for alcohol problems: Findings of the randomised UK alcohol treatment trial (UKATT) *British Medical Journal*, 331, 541.

Visschers, V.H.M., Meertens, R.M., Passchier, W.W.F. and De Vries, N.N.K. (2009) Probability information in risk communication: A review of the research literature. *Risk Analysis: An International Journal*, 29, 267–87.

Webb, T.L. and Sheeran, P. (2006) Does changing behavioural intentions engender behavior change? A meta-analysis of the experimental evidence. *Psychological Bulletin*, 132, 249–68.

Weinstein, A. and Cox, W.M. (2006) Cognitive processing of drug-related stimuli: The role of memory and attention. *Journal of Psychopharmacology*, 20, 850–9.

Weinstein, N.D. and Sandman, P.M. (1992) A model of the precaution adoption process: Evidence from home radon testing. *Health Psychology*, 11, 170–80.

West, R. (2005) Time for a change: Putting the transtheoretical (stages of change) model to rest. *Addiction*, 100, 1036–9.

White, J.M. (1991) *Drug Dependence*. Englewood Cliffs, NJ: Prentice Hall.

Wickler, A. (1948) Recent progress in research on the neurophysiological basis of morphine addiction. *American Journal of Psychiatry*, 105, 329–38.

Wiers, R.W. and Stacy, A.W. (2010) Are alcohol expectancies associations? Comment on Moss and Albery (2009) *Psychological Bulletin*, 136, 12–16.

Wiers, R.W., Beckers, L., Houben, K. and Hofmann, W. (2009) A short fuse after alcohol: Implicit power associations predict aggressiveness after alcohol consumption in young heavy drinkers with limited executive control. *Pharmacology, Biochemistry and Behaviour*, 93, 300–5.

Williams, L.E. and Bargh, J. A. (2008) Experiencing physical warmth promotes interpersonal warmth. *Science*, 322, 606–7.

Witte, K. (1992) Putting the fear back into fear appeals: The extended parallel process model. *Communication Monographs*, 59, 329–49.

Zuckerman, M. (1983) Sensation seeking and sports. *Personality and Individual Differences*, 4, 285–93.

Zuckerman, M. (1994) *Behavioural Expressions and Biosocial Bases of Sensation-Seeking*. Cambridge: Cambridge University Press.

Index

Entries in **bold** refer to glossary definitions

Reading guide

This table identifies where in the book you'll find relevant information for those of you studying or teaching A-level. You should also, of course, refer to the Index and the Glossary, but navigating a book for a particular set of items can be awkward and we found this table a useful tool when editing the book and so include it here for your convenience.

Topic	AQA(A)	Edexcel	OCR	AQA(B)	Page
AA approach		x			117–18
Alcohol				x	4, 10–12, 25, 28, 31–6, 47–8
Attribution	x				79
Biological intervention	x				107
Biological model	x				19
Conditioning		x			57–9, 60–3
Depressants				x	47, 143
Explanations for gambling	x				9, 53, 97–9, 140
Explanations for smoking	x				47, 53, 109–10
Fear-arousal				x	126–8, 130–2
Heredity				x	34–6
Learning model	x				52
Legislation	x		x	x	127, 132
Personality				x	73–6

Topic	AQA(A)	Edexcel	OCR	AQA(B)	Page
Physical dependence		x		x	43, 46
Prochaska model				x	13-14, 65
Psychological dependence	x	x		x	46
Public health interventions	x	x	x	x	126
Reinforcement		x			40, 44 (see conditioning)
Self-esteem	x				126-8, 132, 143-5
Self-management				x	70
Smoking	x			x	47, 53, 109-10
Social factors				x	3, 4, 9, 12, 13, 16, 48
Social learning		x			53, 64-8, 129
Solvent abuse				x	25
Stimulants				x	47, 50, 104
Synapse		x			37-9
Theory of planned behaviour	x				12, 13
Theory of reasoned action	x				12, 13
Tolerance	x	x			3, 4, 6, 7, 21, 42, 61-3
Withdrawal	x	x		x	2, 3, 4 (misc. others throughout)

Printed and bound by CPI Group (UK) Ltd, Croydon, CR0 4YY